Live Your Life for

HALF THE PRICE

Mary Hunt

Revell

a division of Baker Publishing Group
Grand Rapids, Michigan

© 2005 by Mary Hunt

Published by Revell
a division of Baker Publishing Group
P.O. Box 6287, Grand Rapids, MI 49516-6287
www.revellbooks.com

Printed in the United States of America

Revell edition published in 2015

Library of Congress Cataloging-in-Publication Data
Hunt, Mary, 1948–
    Live your life for half the price / Mary Hunt.
        pages cm
    Includes bibliographical references.
    ISBN 978-0-8007-2147-3 (pbk.)
    1. Finance, Personal. I. Title.
    HG179.H8555 2015
    332.024—dc23   2014049449

15 16 17 18 19 20 21   7 6 5 4 3 2

In keeping with biblical principles of creation stewardship, Baker Publishing Group advocates the responsible use of our natural resources. As a member of the Green Press Initiative, our company uses recycled paper when possible. The text paper of this book is composed in part of post-consumer waste.

In your lifetime, you will manage millions of dollars. You are receiving your fortune in installments—one paycheck at a time. The money you don't spend will ultimately give you the freedom to live the life you love.

Contents

Acknowledgments   9

An Interview   11

Introduction   15

1. The Life You Love   19

2. Found Money   31

3. Handy Tools, Secret Weapons   43

4. The Jarring Truth about Food Shopping   69

5. News Flash! There's a Kitchen in Your House   89

6. The Mother of All Budget Busters   103

7. No More Back-of-the-Closet Mistakes   119

8. Attack of the Killer Fees   141

9. Home, Sweet, Paid-for Home   151

Contents

10. Remember When Talk Was Cheap? 165

11. Strategies for Big-Ticket Items 175

12. Your Dream Ride for Half the Price 193

13. Disaster, Disease, Death, and Other Fun Topics 219

14. Travel and Family Fun 239

15. Your Satisfaction Guaranteed 259

16. Rules to Live By 267

Afterword 275

Appendix A 279

Appendix B 323

Notes 335

Index 339

Acknowledgments

I t's been more than two decades since I founded Debt-Proof Living. What an amazing ride. How did I get so lucky? The truth is I didn't get here alone. I've been privileged to have so many people help me on this journey, and I am humbled.

Thanks again to my husband, Harold, who has been right beside me through every dip and turn, always supporting and believing in me. And my kids—Josh, Wendy, Jeremy, and Tawny—what did I ever do to deserve you?

Huge thanks to Raquel Contreras for keeping our home clean so I am free to do what I do better than cleaning house, which is writing. And writing and writing.

I have so many other people to thank: Cheryl Van Andel for her beautiful cover design, Kristin Kornoelje for making these pages so readable and error-free, and most of all my editor and long-time friend Vicki Crumpton for making this book possible.

Thank you to Josh Hunt and Max Halbert for managing the DPL office so I can quietly check myself into book jail from time to time, confident that everything will be well taken care of in my absence.

Last, to you my readers who continue to inspire me every day, thank you!

An Interview

O ver the years, I've had many media interviews, and I'm grateful for every one. One interview, however, stands out in my mind because of an unfortunate case of host laryngitis. It was the first time I'd ever been asked to interview myself. Seriously.

I can't say it was unpleasant. In fact, I rather enjoyed myself. I responded candidly to each of my questions; I knew all the answers and didn't stump myself even once.

Now I find myself in a similar situation. There you are and here I am. I know you have questions, but alas your voice is silent. So what I did that day for a radio audience, I've decided to do for you: I will interview myself.

Me: Why did you write this book? There are plenty of books out there on personal finances already.

Myself: I know this looks like a personal finance book, and it is in a way, but not really. This book focuses on just one segment of the art of managing your money.

Me: You're going to make me ask?

Myself: I wasn't finished. It's the part about limiting your spending so that it does not exceed 80 percent of your income.

Me: Oh, so this is a budget book!

Myself: No, not really.

Me: A bargain guide?

Myself: No, not that either. This is a book about how to live below your means—how to spend less than you earn. Living below your means is a decision, an attitude—it's a way of life.

Me: Forgive me, but I don't understand the difference between living below your means and finding great bargains.

Myself: If you are committed to maintaining a healthy margin between what you earn and what you spend, you're going to be a deal hunter. But the bargain isn't the issue—the bargain is simply the means to the end. The real issue is achieving a lifestyle where you buy what you need and want what you have—a consistent way of life where you live below your means.

Me: Who did you write this book for?

Myself: Since 1992, I've devoted my life to helping people make the shift from spender to saver—showing them how to stop spending all they have, how to get out of debt, and how to live below their means. Millions have taken me up on my offer and proven that my simple debt-proof living plan works.

I can't tell you how many people have gotten out of debt and gone on to do amazing things with their lives and their money. I really can't. I know—and this breaks my heart—that for every success there are ten thousand more who don't get it or, if they do, procrastinate. They make good money and they're not horribly in debt, but they spend all of their money—all the time. These are the people who need this book.

Me: Who would not benefit from this book?

Myself: I'd like to think that I'm such an entertaining writer that anyone would find this a real page-turner, but those who never spend beyond their means, those who give, save, and are building wealth will probably not find much inspiration. They are already doing what I'm talking about here. While I'd be honored if they flipped a few pages, I did not write this for those who are seasoned at living below their means and are looking for ways to go lower and lower. And lower.

Me: So what can we expect in the pages that follow?

Myself: You may have noticed this is a single volume, not a ninety-six-volume matched set. That's why you are not going to find every possible consumer product and service together with details on how and where to buy it for 50 percent off. This is not *Mary Hunt's Guide to Bargains*. I hope to empower my readers to action by teaching them the principles of living below their means and showing them how to reduce the cost of some of their major expenses.

Me: Thanks for being my guest today. Where can our readers find you if they have questions?

Myself: It was my pleasure! These days I spend most of my time hanging out at my website DebtProofLiving.com and my blog EverydayCheapskate.com.

Introduction

Affluence is not measured by your annual income. Affluence is determined by how many of your resources you manage not to spend—the amount of income you keep.

Live Your Life for Half the Price is about how to spend less than you earn, how to make better choices with what you have so you can keep more of what you make. Who should read it? Anyone ready to achieve extraordinary results on an ordinary income.

The idea that you should live below your means is obvious, isn't it? It's not like this is the first time you've ever heard of the concept. You know that cutting spending is hard work but living paycheck to paycheck is much harder work. So if you knew how to stop spending so much, it's safe to say you'd be doing that by now.

Living on less than you earn takes effort. Like swimming upstream or walking up the down escalator, you have to work at going against the flow. It takes a conscious effort to spend less on everything from food to ATM fees, insurance to clothes, and the fun things in life too.

Sadly, by the looks of climbing credit card debt and personal bankruptcy filings in the United States, too few people are willing to put forth the effort. It seems easier to just spend all you have and then depend on credit to cover the gap between what you think you need and how much you make. At the time, it seems fine to have it all now and pay later. Yet, we eventually learn the long-term effects of that spending error.

If you are not where you'd like to be with your money, don't assume that's because you make less money than you desire. Increased income does not guarantee a better life. Think about it. Ten years ago your annual income was less than it is now. Perhaps it was a lot less. You believed then that if you only made more money you'd be out of debt and on your way to building wealth and securing your future.

Then you got a raise or changed careers. Your annual income improved, but then you added new expenses and accepted new debt. Before long, you started thinking again that if you only made more money you'd be out of debt, on your way to building wealth and securing your future.

Then you got another raise or changed careers. You made more money. You took on more expenses, added more debt. I know I am repeating myself, and that is my point. You're caught in a vicious cycle that insists more money is the only way to improve your financial situation.

More money alone is not likely to change your life. You've proven that. Making the decision to stop spending all of it so you can keep more of it—that's the solution.

It took me decades to wise up. But finally I found the key to the life I love. I hope it doesn't take you that long. How much more time can you afford to waste? No matter your current income, you can do better with what you have without giving up the life you love. Just the fact that you are reading these words right now means you have an important resource within your grasp.

As you read this book, make it a personal challenge to see how much of your money you can manage to keep. Make it a game. Try different strategies. Some things will work better for you than others. I ask only that you be open to many options.

I know that with the right information, motivation, and encouragement you can shift your energy from treading financial water to achieving financial freedom. What makes me so sure? For fifteen years, I've been helping people get out of debt. Their success can be directly connected to their personal decisions to live on less—to stop spending everything they make. None of these stories were overnight miracles. It takes time and hard work to right the wrongs of past mistakes and to change behaviors, habits, and attitudes. But it is doable. The stories are amazing.

I am handing you the opportunity to change the course of your life. I am giving you a chance to take charge of your finances, to do better with what you have so you can start making the kind of progress with your money about which you've only dreamed.

And now you have a decision to make. I hope you will grab this opportunity to finally stop living beyond your means—regardless of your income level or current financial situation. You're about to discover you can do more with what you have—more than you dream possible. If you're ready to take on the challenge, so am I.

Let's get started!

The Life You Love

I was asked to interview sixty millionaires from Oklahoma. What I learned from them was simple, yet the message had a lasting impact on me: You cannot enjoy life if you are addicted to consumption and the use of credit.

Thomas J. Stanley, *The Millionaire Next Door*

Shortly after graduating from college, I married the love of my life. We had no debt, but we had new sheets and towels. Life was wonderful. In fact, my life had never been this good. I was finally done with school, I loved my job, and my new husband adored me.

Had you knocked on the front door of our tiny home (three hundred square feet, no kidding) and asked me to rate the quality of my life, I would have given it the highest possible marks without hesitation.

The Card

I got my first credit card for convenience, pure and simple. Harold, my conservative banker husband, did not share my enthusiasm but finally agreed. I didn't see this as a way to build our credit history or spend money we didn't have; I thought it would be more convenient to use this Texaco card and pay the bill once a month than scramble for money every few days to put gas in my car. I would save time too.

The minute my new card came in the mail I took it for a test-drive. For fun, I pulled up to a full-service pump (back when they had those) just as proud as I could be. I felt like royalty because within seconds several attendants addressed my every automotive need.

I felt a sense of privilege I'd never known. It felt good. And with this magic card, I didn't have to worry about a thing, because my husband would take care of the bill.

You don't think the queen of England actually pays her bills, do you? Of course not, and why should I? Privilege. Entitlement. Quality of life. As long ago as this was, I remember the incident as if it happened this morning, right down to what I was wearing. I guess you might say this was one of my life's "defining moments."

Blinded by flawed thinking that suggests if one is good, two must be better, I added several more credit cards to my collection. My quality of life began to improve in other areas, little by little. I couldn't believe all the quality I'd been missing.

Having the freedom to buy stuff whenever I wanted was a big deal to me. I'd grown up with very little. Now, for the first time in my life, I could act on my compulsive urges. No waiting. Just make a snap decision and move on.

We got a new car. We had a baby. Make that two. We bought the best toys. Legos, Star Wars action figures, video games. Then came cool clothes, hobbies, more new cars, and a new swimming pool. Ah, quality of life, standard of living.

Our family vacations and big Christmases added even more to my quality of life. We enrolled the kids in private schools. They participated in sports and other enrichment programs. We even bought a recreational vehicle to improve the quality of our lives. It worked for a while.

We crossed a significant threshold the month we were unable to pay the credit card bills in full. Enter consumer debt.

Debt Turns Ugly

Let me tell you about high-interest, unsecured, revolving credit card debt. It's like cancer. It begins as a single cell, and you don't even feel it.

Opting to pay the minimum payment rather than the full balance was effortless, painless . . . no noticeable negative effect at all. It was easier to pay $40 than $400. Breathing space, relieved pressure. It was like a gift—as if we were getting away with something.

At that point, I would have told you—and meant it with all my heart—that consumer debt improved our lives. It allowed us to do more things and get more stuff. It was like getting a big raise even though our income had not increased.

But like a single cancer cell that begins to multiply, so did our debt. It grew and multiplied until it nearly killed us. We missed payments, incurred late fees, and had to borrow more and more to handle our ever-growing minimum payments. The very thing that had "improved" our quality of life began to eat away at it instead.

By the time we celebrated twelve years of marriage, we were in our third home, our two bundles of baby boy joy were six and seven, and we were driving two fancy new cars. We had changed careers and also tried self-employment.

If I could stop here, you might assume that our quality of life had improved even more remarkably. But lest you jump to that conclusion, let me also tell you that we had amassed more than $100,000 in unsecured (mostly credit card) debt. Things were way out of hand.

We were horribly in debt, and our business had failed. We were unemployed, months behind on our bills, and facing foreclosure on our home. We had no savings, no retirement accounts to cash in, and no rich uncles in the family tree. Let me assure you that there was little quality in our lives.

True Quality

I longed for the simple life in our cozy three-hundred-square-foot home when we got regular paychecks, paid our bills on time, paid cash for our day-to-day living, and had money in the bank. We were so happy then. Our quality of life was authentic. That was the life I loved.

I loathed the trap that now held us so tightly. I discovered too late that having it all now and paying for it later was a hollow promise—a torturous prison. The credit that promised the freedom to have and do anything I wanted now held us in bondage.

I didn't set out to ruin our lives. I didn't sit down one day and dream up a foolproof plan to plunge me and my family into the kind of financial distress from which few recover. I thought I was making our lives better. I was driven by this thing we call "quality of life."

The Pit of Despair

I wish I could say I woke up and came to my senses on my own. The truth is I hit rock bottom so hard that it shook me to the core of my being. Never before or since have I experienced such pain, defeat, and despair.

I had to reach my lowest point, where I could do nothing but let go of my stubborn demands to be in charge of my life. On that day, I humbled myself before God and admitted that I could not fix this. I was out of options. I poured my heart out to God, asking for forgiveness and help. So terribly afraid of losing my husband, my boys, and my home, I promised that day that I would do anything to repair the damage I'd done and repay the debt I'd amassed.

Our journey back is a story for another place and time, but we did make it back. We paid our entire debt without filing for bankruptcy or asking for a single concession from our creditors. Our home did not go through foreclosure, our marriage survives to this day, and our boys are now financially responsible adults.

While it took thirteen years to repay our debt, the quality of our lives began to improve the first day of the journey back. But it was a different kind of quality—authentic and rock solid.

I learned so much on that journey back to solvency. No doubt things can improve the quality of our lives—but only to the extent that we own them and they do not own us. Material things satisfy physical needs. But it takes more than meeting physical needs to find satisfaction and experience true quality of life. We need contentment, joy, and peace of mind too.

Here's what I want you to know and understand. Reducing our spending was the catalyst that started the dramatic and permanent change in our lives. And that change was not limited to our finances. It was all-pervasive. Learning the power of living below our means gave us the life we love. It affected our relationships, our spiritual lives, our home life, our children's lives—and now your life.

May I Ask You a Question?

I have asked many people this question: What contributes to the quality of your life and brings you satisfaction? Typically, I get a blank stare. If I wait long enough, I get a fairly predictable response in the form of a list.

Take a look at the following list of the responses I have received.

all my bills paid
money in the bank
peace of mind
contentment
love
a paid-for home
a fast computer

24

a fine leather handbag
good health
a beautiful quilt
my garden
spending time with my kids
a great meal
my spouse
grandkids
walking in the country
a smartphone
good friends
pets
a week in Yosemite
a massage
a week away anywhere
a warm fire on a cold night
a good book
makeup
great clothes
helping others in need
knowing my purpose
freedom to do what I want

Not surprisingly, all the times I have asked people what brings quality to their lives, no one has responded, "A closet full of clothes I never wear" or "A garage that is so packed with stuff there's no room for a car." No one has mentioned the forty-eight remaining payments on the pair of Jet Skis.

As you read through that list, did you see anything you would place on your list? Would your list fall in line with the one above, or would yours be completely different? What would you add or subtract? There are no right or wrong answers. But I can assure you that making such a list for yourself will be enlightening.

What contributes to the quality of your life? Now take a minute and narrow that to the top ten things that define your quality of life.

Would a Boatload of Money Help?

If you're holding out for the life you love to magically appear once a boatload of money gets dumped into your life, don't count on it.

You may believe in your heart that winning the lottery or getting an unexpected inheritance would make your life perfect. Perhaps you're convinced that getting in on the ground floor of the latest and greatest multilevel marketing opportunity would make you rich overnight. That won't happen.

If you can figure out a way to get that kind of money, good for you. But if you think money alone—and plenty of it—will give you the life you love, forget it. Money alone, no matter how much of it flows through your life, will not automatically materialize into the life you love.

Either you are living the life you love or you aren't. If you are, you may be fearful that reducing your spending or not relying on credit to get by will force you to live a life you hate. That's a real fear, one with which I can identify. After all, if you've never consciously worked at living below your means, the fear of becoming a penny-pinching miser may give you the creeps.

Or if you aren't happy with your life, you may be dreaming about what it would be like to really love your life. You know it's out there, you can imagine what it would be like, but it is forever out of reach. No matter how hard you try or how fast you go, you cannot quite grab on to it. You believe that what stands between you and the life you love is more money. That is probably not the case at all.

Whether you fear losing the life you love or only dream of living it, here's the bottom line: You need to learn how to live on 80 percent of your income. You have to cap your spending at 80 percent of the money you bring home no matter what. Make it a habit as fundamental as stopping for red lights. Realize once and for all that if you can't pay for it today from the money you have, then you can't afford it.

Stuff alone does not make our lives better. Sure, a good computer, a comfortable home, and a reliable car add quality to our lives. But without peace of mind, someone to love, and a good sense of why on earth you are here in the first place, all of that is just stuff. And more of it is just more stuff.

When you started reading this book, I promised you that you can live your life for half the price without sacrificing the life you love. I meant that, and I believe it with all my heart.

Satisfaction Saturation

I'll never forget the time I asked one of my young piano students what he wanted for Christmas. It was a generic question, a pleasantry. I wasn't looking for make, model, and serial number, but that's what I got. He whipped out a sixty-page list from his book bag. I gulped, checked to see if this child was serious (he was), and quickly proceeded with his music lesson.

I don't know how many toys, electronics, and gadgets he had on that sixty-page Christmas list, but five things per page would equal three hundred entries! I'll admit to participating in a few overly indulgent Christmases in my foolish past, but even I cannot imagine what that child's dream Christmas would look like.

Somehow I think that most of us have a bit of that kid in us. We want it all. And every bank and credit card company out there is affirming the notion and willing to make it happen.

In time, however, we reach the maximum level of satisfaction. And the more we attempt to increase that level, the more difficult it becomes to retain a sense of fulfillment. More becomes less as our feelings of satisfaction diminish.

By the looks of some of our closets and garages, we've been doing a pretty good job of trying to get it all. But how much of it satisfies? What portion of what we have is actually contributing to the quality of our lives?

The secret to living the life you love is the ability to identify the point of maximum fulfillment, the point of "enough." More than enough will not increase your happiness; in fact, it will eat away at your sense of satisfaction.

Get in touch with your internal satisfaction meter. Doing this will be very revealing. Rate your possessions. How much satisfaction do they give you? If you consider everything in your life, rating its level of satisfaction, you will learn a lot about yourself and your current situation.

Review, Not Regret

Imagine how different your current financial picture might be had you not spent so much of your past income on stuff and activities that did not improve the quality of your life or, worse, actually diminished your happiness. It makes you wish you'd never purchased anything that wasn't needed or wanted, doesn't it? While I am not suggesting that you should live with regret, a thoughtful review of how you've managed your money up to now can prevent you from repeating the same mistakes in the future.

As you begin to review your possessions through the filter of how they contribute to or subtract from the quality of your life, you will make some startling discoveries. You've been hanging on to things that don't make a positive contribution to your life. They do not serve you, yet they take up space in your world. They keep you from the peace you could be experiencing or, worse, steal your joy.

Living below your means does not mean giving up life's pleasures and what really matters to you. On the contrary, spending less than you earn is the way to have and do those things that will maximize the quality of your life.

Found Money

The bottom line is that we think we work to pay
the bills—but we spend more than we make on
more than we need, which sends us back to work
to get the money to spend to get more stuff to . . .

Joe Dominguez, *Your Money or Your Life*

Money in the bank. Bills paid. No debts. A paid-for
home. A healthy retirement plan. All contribute
to feelings of peace and security. No doubt money plays a
major role in determining the quality of our lives. Still, we
have seen that once our basic needs are met, more money
will not necessarily bring more happiness. Instead, what
we do with our money makes the difference in how we live
our lives.

Finding Money

So here you are, determined to improve the quality of your life by living below your means. The situation seems perfectly clear—you need to find more money. You have two choices: increase your income or reduce your spending.

Option 1: Increase Income

Making more money does seem like the most logical way to fix a financial problem. There are only a limited number of ways to do that.

Beef up your paycheck. You can ask for a raise. You can land a new job that pays a lot more than your current job. Or you can get a second (or third) job to supplement your current income.

Land a windfall. I mention this in case winning the lottery or getting a big inheritance is on your list of realistic options for changing your financial picture. Theoretically, both are options, but I don't suggest you count on either as a realistic way to increase your income. Your chances of being struck by lightning are much better than winning the lottery. As for that inheritance, you be the judge.

Sell assets. Finding a cash buyer for your grandmother's sterling silver, the boat, all the clothes and household items you never use, a piece of real estate, or any other asset you own is another option for increasing your income.

All of these are ways to increase your income and improve your financial picture. But let's get real. If you could do any of these things, you would have done them already and we wouldn't be having this conversation.

While increasing your income is a way to change your financial picture, the change may not be good for you. Believe it or not, increasing your income could worsen your financial position.

Let's say you ask for that raise and (surprise!) get a nice annual increase of $5,000. First, you'll never see the entire $5,000 due to taxes. What you do take home will come in small increments. In addition (I hate to be the bearer of bad news), a raise could push you into a higher tax bracket. Once your impressive raise is subjected to taxes and other withholdings, you'll be lucky to see an extra $60 in your weekly paycheck. Ditto if you work overtime.

Let me point out one more fact. Even if you can start working overtime or arrange for that raise to be effective today, it will take several weeks for you to see any of it. However, any increases in related expenses—additional childcare, gasoline, and other expenses incurred because of additional time away from home—will kick in immediately.

I am certainly not against pay increases. I just want you to be aware of all aspects and the true benefit and cost of a pay increase.

Something else also happens when you get a big boost in income. If you aren't careful, it can encourage increased feelings of entitlement. Suddenly you deserve a new outfit, better birthday parties, a better cell phone, a faster computer, a great vacation, a newer car, a larger house.

Let's say you decide that $5,000 looks like a down payment on a vehicle upgrade. You could sure use a minivan. So you buy one—a great new van with $469 monthly payments. Of course, you do this before you see that $5,000 boils down to $60 a week. You've just worsened your financial situation with new debt and a monthly payment that exceeds your net increase.

You may discover after you've added up your entitlements that your $60-a-week increase doesn't go far. In fact, your increased income has put you further behind.

Let's say that you can find a way to increase your income so that it actually improves your financial situation. Not bad. But here's the problem. Just what exactly caused your money problems in the first place? Overspending? Too much credit card debt?

Your newly enhanced income may do little more than stick a financial Band-Aid on a pile of bad habits. If you fail to address them, nothing will change. In fact, statistics suggest that more money only makes financial problems worse, not better.

Option 2: Reduce Spending

Your other option for improving your financial picture is to systematically, methodically, and intelligently reduce your spending. If you are currently spending $1, you need to find a way to reduce that to 80 cents.

Unless you live below the poverty line—in which case you have a different set of challenges—I am confident that with persistence you can reduce your spending. You can. This effort will have all the positive effects of increasing your income without the challenges mentioned above.

It's instantaneous. Reducing your expenses brings instant gratification. Here's an example. You normally spend $140 a week at the supermarket. This week you spend only $100, which means you have $40 in your wallet for some other use. No waiting and no begging; no loans, no debt, no payback.

Every expense you have—not just your grocery tab—is a candidate for some type of systematic reduction.

Less stress. Assessing the way you spend your money forces you to focus on what really matters. You begin to notice unneeded "baggage." You're more willing to acknowledge what brings you joy, what needs to go, and how to create the life you love. Chaos slips away, leaving calm and simplicity in its place. Reducing your expenses will have a far-reaching effect on more than just the balance in your bank account.

More contentment. Examining what is meaningful and then having the courage to confront the rest will bring a sense of contentment to you and your family. Instead of being so concerned about getting everything you want, you'll find contentment in wanting what you have. Overindulging in stuff complicates life and causes much stress.

The Best Option

I'm sure it will come as no surprise to you that I'm partial to reducing spending over increasing income as the way to improve your financial situation. You knew that all along. The title of this book gave it away.

Earning more money, landing a big windfall, or any other way of increasing one's income is like playing offense. Reducing expenses, on the other hand, is playing defense. And doing it well is great defense.

When it comes to personal finance, choosing to always play offense is exhausting. Playing a great defense is a common attribute in the habits and lifestyles of self-made millionaires.

The majority of adults in the United States live beyond their means, if credit card statistics are the gauge. More than 60 percent of active credit cards carry a balance from one month to the next.[1] That tells me that the cardholder is unable to pay the balance in full in a single month. The debt is greater than the ability to pay.

If you're in this group, you're in trouble, digging yourself into a horrible pit of debt. You're spending your future. Run, do not walk, to the closest copy of my book *Debt-Proof Living*. I'll be there waiting, ready to help you get out of debt.

The 80 Percent Solution

The key to achieving financial freedom is to live below your means—specifically, to limit your overall spending to 80 percent of your net income, to spend only 80 cents for each $1 you see in your paycheck. Impossible? No. It takes skill, effort, and determination. It takes desire and commitment to live below your means—to be fully committed to living the best life you can on 80 percent of your income without sacrificing the life you love. But it's possible.

You may wonder about the other 20 percent of your paycheck. What happens to that? It's all part of a plan that creates the financial balance necessary for living below your means. For each dollar that flows into your life, you give away 10 cents and you put 10 cents into your emergency or contingency fund, as I refer to it. Giving and saving are the magic bullets that will quiet your insatiable desires, put to rest your fears, and give you incentive to live the life you love on 80 percent of your take-home pay.

So you may be wondering how this 80 percent solution squares with half-price living. Studies indicate that only 41 percent of US households spend less than the family brings home from the workplace. Many people make up the difference by charging expenses on their credit cards, placing themselves deeper in debt each month.[2] Let's say that describes you. Here I come suggesting that you should not only stop spending more than you earn but also reduce your living expenses even further to 80 percent so you can start saving money consistently and also become a generous giver. I know. That is an overwhelming expectation, particularly if you are currently struggling while living beyond your means. Now you can see that living your life for half the price is necessary if you ever hope to practice the 80 percent solution.

Don't worry about losing your dignity. In fact, no one needs to know about your new resolve to find ways to drastically cut your expenses. You don't have to print, "I'm cheap!" on your forehead. A better option is to engrave this motto on your mind: Wherever I am, whatever I do, I can find a way to do it for less.

It is unrealistic to think that in order to reduce spending you will never pay full price again or that everything is available somewhere for half price. But if your goal is to spend less than you make and you are willing to work at it, you can drastically reduce your expenses without sacrificing the aspects of your life that mean the most. It will average out over time. This is a mind-set, an attitude.

Your Money Temperament

To loosely assess your money temperament, consider the following premise, then choose the response closest to what you would do.

Your rich uncle gets wind of your desperate need for transportation. In a surprise move, he sends you $15,000 with instructions to buy a car. What do you do?

A. Make a $15,000 down payment on your dream car.

B. Pay cash for a $15,000 car.

C. Exercise extreme patience, flexibility, consumer savvy, and negotiating skills to find a dandy used, late-model, low-mileage, well-maintained car for $7,500 and then stash $7,500 into a savings account.

Putting aside your humble author's obvious bias, let's analyze these options.

Twice the price. If you responded A, you are prone to live your life for twice the price. You don't mind paying interest and monthly payments because that's the way to get what you want. You're just doing the best you can to maximize your income so you can drive the car you desire.

You depend on consumer credit to bridge the gap between your income and your expenses. It's easy and convenient. Because you pay double-digit interest rates on your revolving debt, you end up paying twice, or more, for the goods and services you charge. However, you don't think about paying double. You live for today; tomorrow will take care of itself.

Full price. If your response was B, you are okay with full price. When you have money, you don't hesitate to spend it. You're a cash buyer, not a wheeler-dealer, and you prefer to just pay the asking price. No hassles, no problems. You have a cash mentality. You pay as you go. If you like it, you buy it. If you don't, you wait.

You don't pay attention to price that much. As a result, your income matches your lifestyle. You don't live beyond your means and never carry credit card debt. Still, it takes every penny to pay the bills. You live from one paycheck to the next. It seems as if you can never get ahead.

Half price. If your choice was C, your mind-set is to live your life for half the price. You enjoy the challenge of living below your means; you try to never pay the full price. You get a thrill whenever you beat the system. You earn more than you spend and save the difference.

You know your prices, you're patient, and you know how to pay less than the going price for just about everything. In fact, you pride yourself on living your life for half the price. You live an understated lifestyle and find great satisfaction in being prepared for the unexpected. You live below your means, and that creates contentment, joy, and a financially stress-free life.

Back to reality. Of course, no one pays "twice the price" for everything, nor can anyone be assured of never paying more than half. My point is that with every spending opportunity comes a choice: choose to go into debt, determine not to spend more than you have, or work hard to pay half the price.

Toil and Trouble

A couple hundred years ago, Adam Smith, economist and philosopher, wrote, "The real price of everything, what everything really costs to the man who wants to acquire it, is the toil and trouble of acquiring it."[3]

I'm not trying to fool you into thinking it's a simple thing to live below your means. I'll admit that it is easier to just buy what you want and then switch to credit when you run out of money. That's as easy as walking downhill. Or rolling off a log.

There is a component of toil and trouble in half-price living, and at times it is more toilsome than other choices. In some ways, living below your means is like having a part-time job with this job description: plan, research, wait, negotiate, strategize, compare, and consider.

What better part-time job could you hope for than one where you set your hours, agenda, and pace and you're the boss? The more toil and trouble you choose to contribute, the closer you'll come to living your life for half the price. And don't forget that the "wages" are tax-free because every dollar you manage not to spend is a dollar on which you have already been taxed.

Toil-and-Trouble Factor on Wheels

Remember the $15,000-for-a-car question? Let's revisit the three options, taking into consideration the toil-and-trouble factor.

Buying the new car in option A took all of one hour. It was simple and convenient and, given the fierce competition among new car dealers, probably quite pain-free. The salesperson was more than willing to handle every detail and made the transaction so simple. You didn't even have to think about the full price of the deal. Just knowing you could handle the monthly payment gave you a sense of satisfaction. No toil, no trouble.

Paying cash in option B required diligence to locate the car. Because this was not a new vehicle, add in the time and expense of a trip to the mechanic for a checkup and inspection.

Paying a lot less in the long run for a good car was offset by the toil and trouble this buyer was willing to contribute to the deal.

Finding a cream puff of a car for just $7,500 in option C was even harder work. It took weeks of patience, test-driving, calling, and networking. But all of the toil and trouble paid off when this amazing low-mileage, single-owner, pampered car turned up. And then consider the additional "paycheck" this buyer received in exchange for his toil and trouble: $7,500 in the bank.

Half-Price Mind-Set

While "half price" refers to the cost of things, half-price living is an attitude, a new way of thinking, a learned behavior. Those with this mind-set see a bigger picture and exercise personal discipline and respect for the money they are entrusted to manage.

I hope that what follows will make you excited about what can happen in your life when you begin to live below your means. And if you've already begun the journey, I want to inspire you to do even better.

3

Handy Tools,
Secret Weapons

If you don't make the shift from spender to saver
at some point in your lifetime, you are dooming
yourself to poverty or having to work forever.

Ted Benna, father of the 401(k)

It takes determination not to spend beyond your means.
And it takes even greater strength to stop spending before
you come to the end of your income. Stopping while there is
still a healthy margin between what you earn and what you
spend requires self-imposed limitations. You have to choose
to place a cap on your spending and then stick to it. Sounds
so simple, doesn't it? It's not.

Living beyond your means is the easy way. Almost anyone who can sign a credit slip can do it. Why would anyone choose the more difficult option of living on less? For the payoff, my friend. It is simply fabulous. Living below your means is your best hope to turn your ordinary income into something extraordinary.

In this chapter, I'll describe the tools and weapons you need to successfully and consistently spend less money than you have available. The more determined you are to equip yourself and be willing to use these tools and weapons, the more successful you will be in living your life for half the price.

Handy tools are tangible items—things you need in your possession to help you accomplish specific tasks. Any craftsperson knows that the right tools for the right job make all the difference in a project's outcome. Some of the tools, as you will learn, you can actually hold in your hands. Others you can view on paper or your computer monitor, tablet, or smartphone.

For our purposes, secret weapons are intangibles—attitudes, values, activities, and behaviors required to stand strong against your opponent. Think of these weapons as your armament—the bulletproof attire you need so you can come out a winner.

The big, bad advertising world does everything it can to control your behavior as a consumer—to get all of the money you have now plus a big promissory note for what you will earn in the future. Going into debt, spending beyond your means, being consumed by stuff—all these results prove that you lose and they win.

Consumer advertising encompasses everything from pre-approved credit card invitations you receive in the mail to store sales, television commercials, online offers, flashy ads for new cars, and the entire gamut in between. The ad industry is bent on manipulating your behavior by creating desire and promising fulfillment. You need weapons to protect yourself against this formidable foe and secure your freedom to spend your money in ways that are consistent with your values, not the values that advertisers would impose on you.

By the way, if you happen to be employed in the advertising industry, do not quit your job! I am a huge fan of capitalism and the free-enterprise system. I love the freedom we enjoy that allows merchants to advertise in an effort to compel people to buy their goods and services. I also believe that consumers need to be at least as smart as the merchants who court them. So consider yourself fortunate to have access to the inside scoop. You have a decided edge in building a counterattack.

The Tools

Cash

Cold, hard cash is as powerful a tool as you can hope to find for the task of spending less of your hard-earned money. Living with cash means you carry currency. You use cash to pay for all your day-to-day expenses—gasoline, food, dry cleaning—expenditures that are not tax deductible and for which you do not need long-term proof of purchase.

Adopting a cash lifestyle requires determination because for most people it is so new, so foreign. We are so used to dealing with money's stand-ins—credit cards, debit cards, and checkbooks. If you are not used to living with cash, at first it feels scary or at least wrong. Blame it on the consumer credit industry.

Decades of clever credit card marketing campaigns have finally made believers of a nation of consumers. We believe that carrying cash is not safe, certainly not convenient, and that we'd be foolish to try to live that way. We learned all of this from the very industry that stands to make a fortune if it can convince us to stop paying with cash.

What about safety? Of course, you need to practice caution with cash. You shouldn't carry around thousands of dollars in cash. And you need a reasonable way to keep cash at home (a small home safe is a good investment). But keep this in mind. Far fewer people are mugged for their cash than have their identities stolen through credit and debit card thievery.

The credit card industry knows that people spend more when they pay with a credit card than when they pay with cash. They know because that is how they designed credit cards to work. They promise improved profits to merchants who accept credit cards.

A Visa USA marketing brochure assures merchants, "A recent Visa study of 100,000 QSR (quick service restaurant) transactions showed that customers using payment cards spent an average of 30 percent more than those who paid with cash. Other industry studies suggest that the average increase may be even higher."[1] MasterCard International makes this promise: "Consumers spend more when they're not constrained by cash on hand. You may see increased purchases of higher-margin products as well as specialty items. And customers may visit your store more often."[2]

Spend cash, spend less. It is a simple principle. It hurts to spend cash, so you spend less to avoid the pain. The credit card industry makes clever use of this principle. They offer a money substitute to relieve the pain. And without the pain, it is much easier to spend and spend and spend.

There really is something magical about credit cards. They make money disappear! Here's an example.

Let's say you need groceries. You plan to spend $50. If you walk into the store with $50 cash in your pocket and no backups (credit cards, debit cards, or a checkbook), you cannot spend $51. You have a self-imposed spending cap. You simply cannot go over it. Instantly, you become a different kind of shopper. You are more careful. You compare prices, look for sales. You are not tempted to pick up items impulsively because they look good, because you are focused on what things cost. What a concept!

Okay, now hit rewind. You need groceries. You plan to spend $50. You arrive with a credit card, debit card, ATM card, checkbook, and $2.43. You can't believe all the great sales; the produce is spectacular; the bakery smells divine. Forty-five minutes later, you roll through the checkout with a final tally of $124.37. Whoops. You went over just a little, but it doesn't matter. You have all kinds of backup to pay for the loot.

Cash is a powerful tool in your mission to live below your means because you have to plan ahead and pay attention to how much cash you have with you before you go into a store. Paying with cash is, in fact, a royal pain. That is what's good about it. Paying with cash requires you to think, be aware, and remain engaged. It requires that you exercise personal discipline. The lack of convenience and ease is what makes this tool so effective. If you purposely make it difficult to spend your money, you will spend less of it.

Of course, it is not possible to live with cash only, so do not get rid of your checkbook or your credit card. You cannot mail cash; you should not use cash to pay your bills. You need to pay for online and mail-order purchases with a credit card (not a debit card, as we will discuss later) so as to be protected in the event your order does not show up, is of poor quality, or is damaged. You need your ATM card to access your cash. Each piece of plastic has a place and proper function in your life. But for all of your day-to-day spending opportunities, forcing yourself to be constrained by the cash you have on hand will make a huge impact on how much of your money you get to keep.

Envelopes

Plain, lowly letter envelopes are a handy tool. Now that you are committed to living with cash, you need a simple way to manage it. It's hard to find a better system. Label your envelopes according to your spending requirements (food, gas, dry cleaning, lunches, and so on) and then divide the cash between them.

As you spend, take the money from the appropriate envelope. You'll know it's time to stop spending when the envelope is empty. Could life be any simpler?

Electronic Resources

The days are gone when computer literacy was an option. Whether you own a computer or have access to one (almost every public library these days has computers available for limited use by the public), you need basic computer literacy skills to go along with the hardware—a computer, tablet, or smartphone and the apps to go with it. These skills include accessing the internet, email, and word processing. You will be far more successful living your life for half the price because of the research capability and online resources you have at the click of a mouse.

Financial Software

Knowing where you are with your money will keep you from slipping out of reality. One of the best uses you can make of your computer is to keep track of your money electronically. Add a good financial software program to your computer and learn to use it. This will revolutionize your financial life. It is like hiring a smart assistant.

Mint. This is an automated way to track personal finances and budget your money, and it is free to use at Mint.com. Mint integrates with all major banks and financial institutions, and it's a breeze to add your bank, credit card, and even brokerage accounts to your pass-coded Mint account.

Every time you revisit the Mint website, your financial data gets updated automatically so you know at a glance exactly how much you have in each of your accounts. The website presents your financial information in an easy-to-use way with pretty graphs and all.

Mint is the most popular of all online personal finance management tools, a service you can access with any web browser or mobile device. Mint is ad-supported, but many users say that even the ads add value to a fantastic tool for managing your money.

LearnVest. Designed to appeal to women, LearnVest.com offers an easy-to-use platform that makes it simple to find and manage everything you need. LearnVest allows you to attach all of your finance accounts ranging from savings to checking accounts, investment accounts, loans, credit cards, and mortgages.

This free program watches your spending and other aspects of your overall financial profile and offers suggestions that help you take control of your finances. LearnVest is like an online coach.

YNAB. YNAB stands for "you need a budget," and you do. YNAB is different from the other budgeting tools reviewed here because this software is a download. It's yours for a one-time fee. You install it, and then it resides on your computer's hard drive and not on the developer's website. You don't have to go online each time you use it, nor does it connect to all of your bank accounts. You choose the information you want to input.

YNAB is available for purchase for $60 (a thirty-day trial is available), which means you can start setting up your budget quickly. Install the 32MB program, fire it up, and let it teach you what it knows.

Tutorials at YouNeedaBudget.com introduce you to the basic concepts used by YNAB. During setup, help windows pop up to explain what different boxes and categories mean. Online, you can read about YNAB's method, which teaches four basic principles: (1) give every dollar a job, (2) save for a rainy day, (3) roll with the punches, and (4) live on last month's income.

Mvelopes. Someone was bound to create "electronic" envelopes. A clever and reputable system for managing your money online can be found at http://DebtProofLiving.mvelopes.com. While there is a fee for this service (it works out to as little as $7.40 a month when you sign up for two years), it is certainly worth your consideration. (Note: I have negotiated a lower rate for friends and family members of my company Debt-Proof Living, and you can count yourself as one of that group. If you access using the URL above, you will get a discounted rate whether you sign up for three months, one year, or two. The company offers an excellent demonstration and a thirty-day free trial. Simply use the above URL to find both. I suggest that you take advantage of the trial period just to make sure Mvelopes is right for you.) Mvelopes is not software but rather an online money management service. It is as safe as it is simple to use.

If you have any hang-ups with things mathematical, you need the kind of personal assistance financial software provides. You will love knowing your checking account is always balanced. You can pay your bills online (some banks will charge a fee for this, although some do not) and even track your spending by category to monitor your progress. Financial software can also assist you with setting up a long-term financial plan and preparing for your tax returns.

As trite as it may sound, it is true that if you take care of your money, it will take care of you. When left unattended, money has the odd ability to vanish without a trace. Nothing is quite as expensive as denial.

Automatic Resources

When it comes to managing your money, just about any automatic resource you can arrange will become a powerful tool against spending beyond your means. The secret lies in our ability as humans to forget. This can either work for us or against us.

If you forget to pay your credit card bill, prepare for trouble. If you forget to record several ATM withdrawals, and your wife is at the same time writing checks against the balance in the checkbook register, prepare for an unpleasant surprise and the possibility of a chain of bounced checks.

But on the other hand, if you forget about the $50 you've authorized as a deduction from your weekly paycheck to be deposited into your 401(k), forgetfulness is a good thing. Soon you don't miss the money because you are not used to receiving it. You forget about it.

Arrange to have your house payment or insurance premium automatically deducted from your checking account each month. This benefits you in ways other than ensuring on-time payments: Many mortgage lenders give a preferred interest rate to those who use automatic payment, and some insurers waive fees in exchange for auto pay.

I am a big fan of all things automatic: lawn sprinkler timers, transmissions, washing machines, savings deposits, bill paying, and just about anything else I can arrange. What I don't see I don't miss.

If you're like me (somehow I think we may be alike), you can easily let things slip. I have a tendency to forget. And in these times when paying late on any bill can cause the equivalent of a natural disaster with your credit score, "automatic" creates a safety net. Having things set up to happen automatically has saved my hide on more than one occasion. The power of automatic payments and deposits can do the same for you.

But here is a cautionary note. Forgetfulness and "automatic" are helpful when it comes to making deposits and paying bills, but this doesn't let you off the hook when it comes to keeping a watchful eye on your bank account, your credit card account, invoices, and other statements.

Proper Plastic

I am opinionated—if not biased—in the area of plastic. As opposed as I am to credit card debt, my position on credit cards may surprise you. You need one good, all-purpose credit card. You need only one, two at the most. Let me explain. Credit cards are not inherently bad. On the contrary, used in the right way, a credit card is an important tool. Credit card debt is the problem to avoid!

Think back to when credit cards were first introduced (of course, we are not old enough to remember, but we've heard others speak of those days, right?). They were called "charge" cards. You had to pay the entire balance at the end of the month. No interest accrued; it was a consumer convenience.

Today, American Express is considered by most to be a "charge card" because the balance must be paid in full each month (although now even AmEx has jumped onto the consumer interest bandwagon with cards that allow for minimum payments and big rates of interest). But you as a savvy consumer can use any credit card as a charge card simply by making sure you pay the balance off before any interest accrues and never charging more than you can reasonably pay in a given month.

A good, all-purpose credit card has these primary features: no annual fee, at least a twenty-five-day grace period, and acceptance in many places. Ideally, it also has a low rate of interest, although this is not a primary requirement because you will not carry a balance.

A credit card is a tool. You use it solely for your benefit, which means you get all the benefits without paying for them—no annual fee, no interest. To be accepted in most places, it should be a MasterCard or Visa. When making your selection from those you may already have, always opt for the card you've had the longest.

Your credit limit on your one good, all-purpose credit card is only as important as its ratio to any balance you may carry on it (your goal is to get this to a $0 balance and keep it there). In these days of computer-generated credit scores (you can get your score at MyFico.com for a fee), the ratio of debt to available credit is very important, as is the length of time you've had your credit card. Carrying balances close to your limit will pull your score down, just as maintaining a large space between what you owe and your credit limit will improve your score.

Many people also have a debit card. You do not need a debit card. A debit card does not carry the consumer protection afforded by federal law the way a credit card does. If a thief gets ahold of your MasterCard- or Visa-branded debit card number, that thug has all he needs to clean out your bank account and every account attached to it. While your bank might have some kind of protection against fraudulent use of your debit card, it is not required by law to do so. And bank provisions can be changed at any time. Even if there is some kind of plan in place to protect you, you may have to prove you weren't the one who went on a major spending spree (remember, you can use a debit card online without producing a PIN or signature).

Finally, in these times when banks charge a fee to speak with a teller (can you even believe that?), you need an ATM card to have fee-free access to your cash or to make deposits. Many banks have eliminated the lowly ATM card in favor of a MasterCard- or Visa-branded ATM/debit card. I'm sure that by now you can figure out their reasoning. While you need ATM access, you don't need a debit card. Finding a bank that offers a simple ATM card may be worth your while.

Credit Score

Your credit score (also known as a FICO score) is a three-digit number that determines the interest rate you will pay on your credit cards, car loan, and home mortgage. It also determines whether you can get a cell phone or rent a home or apartment. A low credit score translates into paying higher interest rates on cards, loans, and insurance premiums; it can even affect your ability to get a job. You live in a world where your credit score is considered a direct reflection of your character.

Your credit score is based on your spending and bill-paying habits and your overall debt load. As such, two of the most important factors are the age of your credit card (how long you've had it) and the ratio of the debt balance (if any) to your available credit. Your current balance should be no more than 30 percent of your available credit to get the optimum credit score.

Tracking

Before I describe this tool (or is it a weapon?—you be the judge), let me tell you why it is so important. You need to know where all of your money goes. If you are part of a couple, this applies to you collectively.

For most of us (I have a feeling there are far more natural-born spenders than those born with that rare "savers gene"), money comes into our lives and is gone so fast that we don't have a clue what really happened to it. The simple act of carefully tracking spending will give you the power of truth in your life versus what you imagine.

Tracking simply means counting—writing down how you spend your money. If two of you spend the household income, both of you should keep this kind of daily record.

While you can use a smartphone or other electronic device, all you really need is a small notebook. Keep it simple and you'll improve your chances of sticking with it. Start each morning with a fresh page. Put the day's date at the top, then write down each purchase made that day (gasoline, coffee, rent, new Jag . . . whatever) followed by the amount. Do this for every transaction, even the small ones, even the secret ones and embarrassing ones. If you spend it, record it. At the end of the day, put that day's record into a drawer or other safe place. The next morning, start with a new page. Repeat the process every day for an entire month. At the end of your first month of tracking, you will be a lot smarter than when you started. You will have a new vision.

And then you will have a job to do. Pull out your month's worth of daily spending records. Categorize all of your spending. Don't make this more difficult than it is. You should be able to see ten to fifteen areas of spending (groceries, fast food, clothing, utilities, housing, transportation, and so on). Don't assume this single month will give you an exact picture of your normal monthly spending. Many expenses do not repeat every month. Still, this is an excellent way to get a feel for how you are spending your money.

Don't be surprised, but do be encouraged, when you see that without doing much more than simply writing down how you spend your money you are becoming a more careful spender. This alone starts you on the path to living your life for a lot less.

Simply seeing where the money goes has an awakening effect on most people, encouraging them to keep more of what they earn. But the real value of this initial exercise is that it allows you to make changes for the coming month. Areas of spending that are really out of control can be tamed by deciding ahead of time how much to spend in that category and then capping it. When you reach the limit in an area, no more spending!

Creating a written spending plan will be as useful as, if not more than, tracking your spending. But nothing will do you more good than exercising the personal discipline to both track and plan.

The Secondary Market

Gently used, previously owned, secondhand, and consignment all refer to the secondary marketplace of consumer goods. In this country of affluence and abundance, the secondary market is huge—bigger than I ever dreamed before the advent of the internet.

Secondary does not always mean the commodity has been used or worn. All it means for our purposes is that it was purchased originally and is now being sold for a second time and at a tremendous price reduction. While I am hesitant to make any promises I cannot keep, I am nearly certain that I could locate just about anything in the secondary market and buy it for a fraction of the new price. It is amazing what is available in this country if you are patient and willing to work hard to find it.

If you decide to participate in the secondary market, you need to find your comfort zone. Some people are more sensitive to the subject of buying used than others. However, the secondary market refers to much more than shopping in thrift stores and frequenting garage sales.

Consignment stores are popping up all over the country— offering everything from baby clothes to designer furniture.

With the added competition comes higher standards. Many thrift stores have become more upscale in an effort to stay current and relevant to their more discriminating customers. These days it is not uncommon to find brand-new items in the secondary market, especially with the explosion of online auction sites.

Now let me warn you. The secondary marketplace offers as many opportunities to overspend as any shopping mall or online shopping opportunity. Just because you find something in excellent condition at an unbelievable price does not mean you need it or should buy it.

While there are plenty of internet online auction sites[3] (OnlineAuction.com, eBid.com, ePier.com, WeBidz.com, WebStore.com, to name a few), eBay.com remains the most popular place to buy and sell. Imagine every antique store in the country together with the contents of every individual's garage and attic all assembled under one roof. That's a small picture of eBay.

Almost everything shows up in the secondary market eventually, and when it does, you'll see it on eBay. Whether you want to know what your grandmother's antique Gorham figurine is worth or where to find the companion piece, eBay is an amazing resource for discovering the current value of anything in the secondary market. It is also dangerous. You can go broke loading up on other people's junk.

If you do not need something specific, do not log on to eBay. This is a dangerous place for a compulsive shopper who has no specific need or does not have the personal discipline to get in and get out.

If you find the item you are looking for, don't make a bid until you first meet the seller. Send this person a friendly email. Confirm the cost of shipping and handling. While your inquiry is sincere, learning the answer is not your primary purpose in making the contact. You want to find out with whom you are dealing. Is this an individual or a big commercial clearinghouse for junk? Be brief and kind. If you do not receive a cordial response within twenty-four hours, you may be dealing with a large merchandiser, not an individual. That could be a red flag, so proceed with caution. Do not continue if you have any doubts or misgivings.

Read the seller's feedback to learn about others' experience with this seller. Negative feedback? Move on. If everything looks positive, look at the seller's number of completed auctions. One seller I tried to communicate with had more than 58,000 completed auctions with a 94 percent positive rating. Six percent may not seem like an unreasonable rate until you realize that means 3,480 unsatisfied buyers. I never received a reply. I learned later that this company buys carloads of returned, damaged, and worn items from major retailers. Too risky for me.

Next, calculate the shipping cost. This is part of the purchase price. Always look at the cost of shipping before you do anything else. Many sellers pad the shipping cost beyond reason. Do not be swayed by a seller who offers, for example, new lamps for 99 cents with no reserve (a reserve price is the minimum price a seller is willing to accept for the item). What's the trick? The shipping/handling fee is $50, something a bidder might miss in the frenzy to get a lamp for a buck. You must include the cost of shipping when considering the full price of the item.

Then check the primary market. Before you make a commitment to buy, make a quick search with a shopping "bot" that will scour the internet to see if you are about to pay too much. Frequently, items are priced higher on an auction site than they cost new elsewhere. There are several shopping bots, such as Google Shopping, Shopzilla, and Nextag. If what you are looking for is available elsewhere on the internet, it will pop up here together with the price. You don't want to pay more for an item on eBay than it costs to buy it new elsewhere. That happens frequently, so buyers beware.

If everything checks out and you decide to make a bid, determine the most you are willing to pay for the item, including shipping and handling, and stick with it. If the bidding goes beyond your limit, walk away. It is easy to keep bidding because you are determined to win.

The Weapons

Your Attitude

The most powerful weapon you have against spending all that you have is your ability to control your thoughts and responses to every circumstance in your life. Think about it. Your attitude is the only thing over which you have complete control. It is more important than education or experience, more important than how much money you have, how much you owe, what you would like to do, or where you want to go.

You cannot tailor the circumstances of your life, but you can tailor your attitudes in response to them. The way you choose to respond to your circumstances—from the mundane to the major—can change the course of your life.

Here are some ideas for putting your attitude to work for you.

Get angry! If you have consumer debt, you know it's the pits. Debt eliminates your options, keeps you awake at night, and can make you lie to your creditors—even to your spouse. I know; I've been there.

So what are you going to do about it? Whine, complain, continue feeling sorry for yourself? I have a better idea. Get mad! Decide once and for all that you will not sell your soul to the likes of MasterCard and Visa—not one more day, not one more purchase. Get righteously indignant at the very idea of transferring your future wealth to creditors. Repeat after me: I've had it, and I'm not going to live on credit anymore!

If you do not have debt, you can still be angry about how it has affected your life. You pay more for things because of consumer debt. Millions of people file for bankruptcy every year, and that affects how much you have to pay to live your life.

Campaign. Think of your attitude as your personal ad agency, public relations firm, and marketing organization all rolled into one. Flood your mind with so many compelling messages of hope and encouragement that no space remains for doubt and discouragement.

Be content. Choosing to be content doesn't mean you toss out your goals and dreams. Contentment is not complacency but rather a decision to enjoy what you have. Contentment is the way to deal with self-pity and other destructive behaviors. Contentment is the equivalent of an emotional massage. It feels that good.

Be grateful. The simple act of choosing to be grateful for what you have rather than focusing on what you don't have is powerful beyond words. Thankfulness is an antidote for the negative attitudes of greed, anger, and fear. Gratitude is a choice that builds a layer of insulation around your life, protecting you from focusing on what you don't have.

Visualize. Create a "mental camera" and keep it with you at all times. When faced with a situation or decision, step out of the picture and look at it through your mind's camera. Zoom out slowly to see this circumstance in the light of tomorrow or the coming week. This will give you a new perspective—more realistic than a close-up view that considers only the moment. Pull away even farther so you view an entire month, then a year. What impact will the decision you make now have on the big picture? Choosing to control your attitude by viewing things in a new way will help you make better decisions.

Isolate. If you are easily dissatisfied or prone to impulsive behaviors, identify your weak spots so you can avoid them. Turn off the television. Skip past the magazine ads. Isolate yourself from mindless shopping. Avoid places you are most likely to slip back into your old ways of spending beyond your means.

Use self-talk. Get into the habit of having heart-to-heart talks with yourself. This is effective in stopping mindless spending. Ask yourself questions before making a purchase of any significance. Then expect honest answers from yourself:

Do I need it?

Do I want to dust (dry clean, insure, store, fuel, maintain) it?

Don't I already have something that will do just as well?

Could I borrow it from a friend or family member?

Is this a good value?

Do I have the cash to pay for it?

How many hours will I have to work to pay for it?

Could I possibly delay the purchase for a few weeks? Months?

Am I willing to wait twenty-four hours before acting?

The single greatest money-saving strategy I've learned over the years is this: When I run across something I think I have to own, I just wait a little while.

Knowing Prices

As simplistic as it might sound, knowing what things cost is one of the most useful weapons against all the forces that conspire to separate you from your money. To not know how much things cost is to be in denial.

Denial is a terrible thing. It tells us that the full price doesn't matter as long as we can handle the monthly payment or as long as there's room on the credit card. Denial says it's cool not to pay attention to price tags—that somehow this indicates a carefree, fabulous way of life where money is no object. But all of that is hogwash. Price does matter, and people who actually have money know what stuff costs. They memorize prices. They are not tricked by sales or specials.

On the other hand, people who live beyond their means prefer not to know what they are spending. It's just easier that way. So know your prices and focus on what things really cost. This practice keeps you engaged and aware. Knowledge is an important weapon, so start paying attention.

The Power of No

At times, your most valuable weapon of all is the willingness to simply exercise good old-fashioned personal restraint—the power to say no!

I have a theory that those of us born with the overspending gene don't overspend on $5,000 designer bags or $1,000 jars of wrinkle cream. Instead, the bargains get us. And the really great bargains really get us.

Just because you can get something for half price doesn't mean you should buy it. It takes a powerful weapon—the power of no—to step away from the bargain, even if buying it would not require you to go into debt.

Discovering ways to radically reduce the cost of your lifestyle could prompt you to buy twice as much just because you can. That not only would defeat the purpose but also would be foolish.

Various forces and temptations will attempt to sabotage your efforts to not spend all of your money. Clever marketing and enticing advertising campaigns will appear to offer authentic ways to help you save more. The ability to say no is powerful beyond words.

The Courage to Negotiate

You may believe negotiating means asking for a discount or haggling with a seller. You're right, but it is more than that. Negotiating is the way you get what you want. Everything is negotiable, whether a major purchase, a larger discount, a better price, getting your teenage son to put the seat down, or receiving a refund on a product or service that did not meet your expectations.

In fact, you are already a negotiator. You negotiate with your kids, spouse, boss, coworkers, employees, creditors, vendors, friends, clerks, and salespeople. You negotiate with telemarketers, repair people, teachers, and neighbors. You negotiate using your words, your tone, your body language, even your silence.

The goal is not that everyone comes out an equal winner but that everyone walks away satisfied. Negotiating a deal that gives something of value to each party is the mark of a wise negotiator.

The point here is to ask for more than you are willing to settle for. To illustrate, let's say you want to make an offer on a house, an offer considerably less than the asking price. You write the offer but in a surprise move stipulate that the price includes the laundry room appliances, pool table, dining room suite, and piano that you saw on your initial tour. The seller responds that the price of the house is acceptable, "But that certainly does not include the personal property!" You win because you get your price (you didn't really want the twenty-five-year-old stuff anyway), and the seller wins because he stood firm against what he considered an unreasonable request.

The person with the most knowledge wins. Never forget that knowledge is power. The more you know, the better your chances of getting what you want. The true skill comes in keeping what you know to yourself and revealing only a bit at a time and only when doing so is to your advantage. Remember that negotiating is a game, and the most skilled player usually wins.

Also, the least motivated party is in control. If the other party finds out how desperate you are to make the deal, you've just lost power. Anytime you can send nonverbal cues that you are not desperate—that you are willing to cancel if you do not get what you want—you retain control. This drives a desperate opponent crazy! No matter how anxious you may be on the inside, never let it show. The simple act of calmly and slowly closing (never slamming) a notebook, briefcase, purse, calendar, newspaper—whatever is handy—is an effective negotiator's most powerful tool. Without saying a word, you send a message that fills your opponent with worry that you are going to walk away.

You need to learn these basic negotiating skills to become an effective negotiator:

1. Prepare. Do the research. Carefully formulate exactly what you want.

2. Set limits. Know in your mind exactly how far you are willing to go and stick with it. This allows you to focus on your alternatives and keeps you from appearing desperate.

3. Create emotional distance. Stick to the facts. Put your emotions away. Never utter the words *feel* or *feelings* in a negotiation.

4. Listen effectively. Remember what your mother always told you about the reason you have two ears and one mouth. No one knows better than I how easy it is to focus so intently on what you want to say next that you fail to really hear what your opponent is saying.

5. Communicate clearly. Choose your words carefully, express them succinctly, and then be quiet. Silence is a good thing. In fact, the first party to break the silence is likely to lose the negotiation.

6. Always remain a fragrance. No matter how things go, remain kind and respectful so that your presence is fragrant. You never want to become an odor.

There you have it—the tools and the weapons you need to begin moving forward with living below your means. But just like the tools in a workshop or the weapons in an arsenal, they are only as good as your willingness to pick them up and use them.

Refer to this chapter often as you pick up one tool after another and rely on these weapons as the need arises. They will give you the power to better manage your money so you can keep more of it.

The Jarring Truth about Food Shopping

How come the odds of going to the store for a
loaf of bread and coming out with ONLY a loaf
of bread are three billion to one?

Erma Bombeck

Food prices in the United States have climbed so dramatically in recent months that a stroll through the aisles of a typical supermarket is enough to kill your appetite. If that was the only place we spent our food dollars, that would be one thing. But most families these days spend as much eating out as they do on food to prepare at home.

The food expense for the typical family—food in all of its forms—is the second-highest monthly expense, second only to housing. According to the USDA, as of January 2014, the cost of food prepared at home for a family of four was $879 a month.[1] Because food is such a huge financial area, eating up so much of your income, we will break this down into several chapters. This chapter is devoted entirely to the challenge of cutting the cost of groceries to half price.

If price were the only criterion for reducing the cost of groceries, the possibilities would be endless, starting of course with a garden and some well-chosen, highly productive farm animals.

Another option for slashing the cost of groceries would be to spend days on end going from store to store, town to town, picking up each and every store's special of the week. I don't have the time or the gasoline for that, and I'm guessing you don't either. What we need is an easy, efficient plan for grocery shopping that meets the following criteria:

1. Takes no more than two hours a week.
2. Does not require that I shop at multiple stores each week.
3. Does not require that I buy store brands.
4. Includes a wide variety of name-brand, high-quality, nutritious foods that cover the USDA's current food pyramid and are family friendly.
5. Does not require that I buy in bulk quantities that are difficult to handle and cause a storage problem in my home.
6. Is cost effective. I decide how much I am going to spend each week, and that amount may change depending on my circumstances.

Tall order? Yes, but fortunately you can accomplish all of this realistically while slashing the cost of your groceries to half the price. However, this requires that you trade in your old way of thinking and open your mind to a new way of food shopping.

But first let's dissect this activity known as grocery shopping.

Two Methods of Grocery Shopping

There must be dozens of ways to shop for groceries, and I'm certain I've tried them all. But when it comes right down to it, every possible method falls into one of two categories: needs shopping or reserve shopping.

Needs shopping is when you buy what you need now at the best price possible and enough to last until you go shopping again.

Reserve shopping is when you buy what's on sale even if you don't need it now so that you don't have to overpay for it when you do need it. Reserve shopping is the process of building a small in-house grocery store. When it's time to make dinner, you visit your own store.

Needs shopping is, in my opinion, a flawed system. Even the most diligent needs shopper—who shops with cash, builds the week's menus around what's on sale, and is careful to avoid all impulsive purchases—will eventually need something that is not on sale. That's what the stores count on. When you pay full price for some of the items in your cart, the store's plan works. They win. Mission accomplished.

Consider this needs-shopping dilemma. You need mayonnaise. The best price today is $3.99 a quart for the store brand. You need it; you buy it. It's not a horrible deal, but it's not great. Four weeks ago at the high-priced supermarket across town where they do crazy things like double coupons to attract shoppers, the quart size of Hellman's mayonnaise was on sale for two for $5. That same week there was a $0.75 manufacturer's coupon for Hellman's mayonnaise in the Sunday paper.

Here's the way that deal would have played out had you been aware of the sale and clipped that all-important coupon: $2.50 for one quart, less $1.50 for the coupon ($0.75 x 2 = $1.50). Final price for the Hellman's: $1. That beats your store-brand deal by 66 percent. And you could have purchased more than one. And had you been diligent to get a couple of those $0.75 coupons when they were available, you could have duplicated the $1 final price a few times.

As a needs shopper, this is your dilemma: You didn't need mayonnaise a month ago. You need it now. The coupon has long expired, and the sale is over. So you pay $3.99 for the off-brand mayonnaise because that's the best deal at the time you need it. To make matters worse, you discover that your friend, a reserve shopper, bought three quarts of Hellman's for $1 each and won't have to restock until it goes on sale again.

Reserve shopping is the best way I know to consistently pay less than half price for name-brand groceries. This method requires a minimal investment of time and energy, but it's a reliable system—you can count on it to work for you week after week. You will enjoy a wide variety of foods in all of the food groups, including meat, produce, and dairy, and it also works for household cleaning products and personal care items.

As a reserve shopper, rather than coming up with menus before you go shopping, you look to the store's sales cycles to determine your food purchases. You create menus after the fact once you go shopping in your pantry's grocery stockpile.

Reserve shopping is an ideal grocery method for singles, families with kids, big families, little families, seniors with no kids—for all situations. You are not locked into narrow selections but have lots of freedom to choose the foods you want to buy. The amount of food is limited by the amount of money you wish to spend. You simply spend up to that limit and stop.

Eventually, you will have a month's worth of basic groceries on hand. This insulates you against wild price fluctuations at the grocery store. You won't find yourself running to the store for one or two things, forced to pay the highly inflated full price.

When challenges come your way—you lose your job or get sick, there's a blizzard, you're hit with unexpected car repairs—with food in the pantry, hard times are less hard.

Create a Price Book

Knowing the everyday and various sale prices of items you buy regularly is important no matter which method of grocery shopping you embrace. You need a practical way to track this important information. Creating a price book unique to your shopping habits and your particular store(s) is an effective way to do this.

If you frequent several stores (for example, the grocery store in your town that has the lowest overall price, the supermarket that doubles coupons, a bakery outlet store, and a produce stand), list in your price book the prices of the items you buy regularly at each of these stores. It's possible you live in a more rural area where you have no choice—it's the one food market in town or nothing. Still, you need a reliable way to track prices.

Let's say the high-priced supermarket has whole-grain bread regularly priced at $3.29 on sale, buy one get one free. You also have a $1 manufacturer's coupon for that item that the store will double. According to my math, with that deal you can buy two loaves of high-quality bread for $0.65 each. The best price you've ever seen in your bakery outlet store is $0.99, and that was a long time ago. Without this valuable information in your price book, you might walk right past an excellent bargain.

Now I have no doubt that you can create a perfect price book on your own, but just in case you need ideas and inspiration, here are resources for your consideration:

- Organized Home offers free printable pages to create a price book (http://organizedhome.com/printable/household-notebook/price-book).
- It's Your Money (MoneySpot.org) offers a free downloadable price book using Excel, which allows you to track the prices of commonly purchased items. This particular tool calculates price per weight unit, price per quantity unit, and price per use if applicable.
- Dollar Stretcher (Stretcher.com) offers a price book with pocket pages and a calculator for $14.95 plus shipping and handling.
- Cheap Cooking (CheapCooking.com/pricebook.htm) has a terrific Excel spreadsheet you can copy to create your price book.

I Have a Confession . . .

I used to be a fanatic needs shopper. And I didn't keep that to myself. In my early books and also my Debt-Proof Living newsletter (formerly Cheapskate Monthly), I advised my readers to shop with cash and to buy only what they needed.

While I'm confessing, let me also say that I was a coupon snob. I could not be bothered with clipping and filing coupons. I tried it once, and it gave me a rash. I am not an organized person. Coupons get lost in the bottom of my purse. They give me a headache. I had a long list of good reasons why clipping coupons was a waste of time and money.

In 2001, as a kind of research project, I set out to prove my position. I couldn't do it. As a result of that experiment, I converted to reserve shopping and remain an avid fan to this day.

One last confession: I do not keep a price book, and I do not track grocery prices. Some people are naturally gifted in the area of data collection and mathematics. I am not one of them.

Objections and Misgivings

Before telling you exactly how reserve shopping works (my method of choice) and how to become a reserve shopper, I want to address the objections and misgivings you may have about this way of buying food.

I will spend more money reserve shopping.
On the surface, this does make sense, but it is not the case. You first need to determine your grocery spending limit. If it is $100 a week, be firm and do not exceed that amount even

if that means leaving bargains at the store. Your stockpile will grow slowly at first, and that's perfectly acceptable.

I will need a lot of extra storage space.

You'll be surprised how many places you have already where you can store your reserve. Nonperishable items can be stashed just about anywhere—under a bed, under the staircase, in the garage or basement. A single cupboard or closet devoted to your food reserve is all you need. I predict in no time you'll be sizing up a broom closet for shelves or clearing space in a cupboard currently filled with stuff you never use.

I will need a freestanding freezer.

Again, not true. The freezer space in your refrigerator is sufficient to handle your frozen reserves. Just make sure to empty, clean, and reorganize your freezer at least monthly. And keep in mind that only a portion of your grocery stockpile will be frozen.

It takes a lot of time.

Once you get the hang of it, you will spend no more time reserve shopping than you do now as a needs shopper. It could be less because you will visit only one store weekly. Just think of all the time you will save when you cut out those last-minute runs to the store for one or two things.

How to Reserve Shop

This is a perfectly legal and ethical way to pay less than half price for groceries—and to do so consistently week after week after week. I mention this only because once you understand how it works and why it works, it seems too good to be true. You know what they say about that. It usually is. But not this time.

This shopping method utilizes these tools: a supermarket's weekly ad and two coupon circulars from the biggest Sunday newspaper in your area. These coupons are published by Red Plum (RedPlum.com) and Smart Source (SmartSource.com) and inserted into all major newspapers in the US. That's all the coupons you need. More may send your brain into serious overload.

Each week, go through the store's ad using your method of choice (more on this follows) and make a list of the sale items priced low enough to be worthy of your business. Next, find the coupons that match those items. You're ready to head to the supermarket.

To be successful at this kind of shopping, a person needs to be organized, somewhat gifted with numbers, and a whiz when it comes to tracking a store's sale cycles. Sadly, I possess none of those qualities. Still, I am proud to say that, in spite of my lack of mathematical and organizational skills, I have built and maintained an amazing stockpile of groceries for many years now.

I have so many groceries in my stockpile that I provide lunch for my entire office staff at least three times a week. I took two months off from grocery shopping recently because the stockpile had grown too large and I needed to pare down. (What could you do with two months of grocery money if you didn't have to use it to buy food?) Over the years, we've also given away loads of food to help people going through difficult times.

You want to know my secret, don't you?

Get Help

I have help. You can have help too. Here's the way I look at this. Why do the tedious work of keeping track of prices and sale cycles—work that makes me crazy—when others are more than willing to do that for me?

I want to introduce you to two websites owned by two smart women who do this work and then let me have a copy of their shopping lists. While both of these websites offer a similar service, they are quite different. Moreover, one site requires a membership fee; the other is free and open to the public.

Thanks to this help, I don't have to do the dirty work. And I routinely walk out of the supermarket with savings of at least 50 percent. My all-time high was a whopping 74 percent savings.

THE GROCERY GAME

Every Saturday, I go to TheGroceryGame.com to get "the list." This is more than a listing of all of the items that are on sale at my supermarket this week (that list would be so long it would take too much paper to print). The list I'm after is the one that identifies the sale items that are an authentic sale—not fake sales trying to trick me.

Let me explain the difference between a real sale and a fake one using General Mills Cheerios as an example. A 15-ounce box has a regular price of $4.29. If you track that one item over the course of a year, you'll have a graph that looks like a wild roller-coaster ride.

One week the price drops to $3.99, then the next week it's down to $2.49, then it's back to $4.29 for a few weeks. Then one week it plunges to $2. That's when it shows up on the list because that's an authentic rock-bottom price. I have a

50-cent coupon for Cheerios that when doubled makes my net price $1. One dollar! I just wait patiently until the list tells me it's time to buy. The only reason I have the luxury of waiting is that I've done the same thing in the past, so we have plenty of cereal at home in our food storage area.

The Grocery Game tracks and offers the list for nearly every supermarket chain across the country. Members invest thirty minutes to one hour each week preparing for their shopping trip and come out with an average of 67 percent savings. A subscription is $10 for eight weeks. A four-week trial membership is available ($1 for four weeks) and highly recommended. Go to TheGroceryGame.com for more information and to sign up for a trial membership.

COUPON MOM

Coupon Mom is every grocery shopper's fondest dream come true. The website is completely free and requires no registration or log in. You could go there right now if you weren't busy reading this book.

When you do go to this site, look for your state and click on a grocery store chain. You'll see a list of the current week's "Best Deals," including the coupon you need to match with it to get an even better deal. Prepare to be amazed. But it doesn't stop there.

While Stephanie Nelson, the Coupon Mom and founder of the Cut Out Hunger program, is eager to help you cut your grocery bills in half, she has another agenda. Her mission is to feed the hungry. She sees so many unbelievable bargains each week (many items you can pick up for just 25 cents if you have the right coupon) and encourages those of us who use the information on her site to donate at least one item from our weekly grocery trek to a food pantry or other charity in our local communities. She will even help us find donation locations.

Can you imagine what could happen if every person in the US who grocery shops any given week were to donate one item to help feed the hungry? We could wipe out hunger in this country and create such amazing reserves that charitable organizations would beg us to stop. Narrow that to just the people in your neighborhood, church, or school group. In very little time, you would be helping individuals and families through difficult times.

Do It Yourself

If neither of these resources applies to your situation—or you simply prefer to track your grocery store's data on your own—here are the steps.

1. *Select a supermarket.*

For optimum stockpiling, you want to shop at the pricey big-name chain supermarket in your area that accepts and hopefully doubles manufacturer's coupons. Supermarket chain stores such as Kroger, Publix, Thrift Way, Frys, Smith's Safeway, Vons, Pavilions, Ralph's, King Soopers, Winn-Dixie, Shoprite, and Albertsons are great candidates. If there are no stores that double coupons in your area, that's okay. This method will still work for you.

High-priced supermarkets are the best place to reserve shop because, while the regular prices are much higher than prices at other stores, their sale prices come in consistently lower. And when matched to a coupon, the net price of the items you buy will consistently beat the cheapest no-frills store in town.

Remember, the supermarkets do all they can to appear to be the cheapest source for groceries in hope that you will pay full price for many of the items in your grocery cart. It doesn't take many full-price purchases in a high-priced store to wipe out a lot of hard work.

2. *Know your prices.*

This is critical. To achieve dramatic savings, you have to be a price wizard, knowing both the regular prices and the various sale prices of the items you buy. Supermarkets are clever. They know shoppers are impressed by sales. But many sales are teasers. You'll need to track prices for a while to discover the sale cycles and patterns. Your detailed price book or database will let you know when the sale price is at its lowest. That's the time to stock up.

3. *Collect coupons.*

Every Sunday, rescue those two coupon circulars from the biggest newspaper in your area (published by Red Plum and Smart Source and inserted into all major newspapers in the US). That's all the coupons you need.

4. *Match sale prices with coupons.*

Once an item is on sale at its lowest price, match it with a coupon and make your buy. And buy as many as you can at that price according to the number of coupons you have for it, the store's policy on multiple coupons, and your financial condition. Then watch your stockpile take off.

5. *Stick to your spending limit.*

Stockpiling can run amok for the compulsive shopper who is driven to buy good deals. You must set a spending limit and be willing to leave bargains in the store once you have reached that limit. Spending twice as much because you are stockpiling makes you an overspender. No matter what, that's not good.

Organize Coupons

Whether you depend on one or both of the grocery list services mentioned on pages 78–79—or you create your own list—the one job likely to drive you nuts is organizing your coupons.

Reserve shopping done well requires that you manage hundreds of coupons—and keep them until they expire but not one day longer. Okay, it's not that critical, but you want to purge often. When you need a particular coupon, you don't want to spend hours trying to remember where you filed it.

Make the Transition

If you are a needs-based shopper wanting to transition to the reserve method, there is an easy way to do so. It will take you about twelve weeks to make the switch and compile a respectable stockpile.

First, identify the supermarket where you will do your reserve shopping. If you have a supermarket in your area that doubles coupons, that should be your store of choice.

Begin to make some stockpiling purchases each week, making sure you buy only items that are at rock-bottom prices and for which you have a coupon. Consider using one of the grocery list services described on pages 78–79 as a resource to help you determine which items are the best deals and which coupons to use.

Continue to make your needs purchases at a no-frills, cheap store. Each week, your needs will diminish and you will begin to shop from your stockpile. After twelve weeks, you will have a well-rounded stockpile. You're on your way.

Use Supermarket Alternatives

Under most circumstances, you will do reserve shopping at a single supermarket. However, you can certainly build and maintain your stockpile from just about any place that sells food. Since each situation is unique and every area of the country offers different options, you have to assess all of your options and then determine what is best for you. There is no one-size-fits-all plan.

No-Frills Grocery Stores

Stores like Food 4 Less, Hy-Vee, Pak'n Save, and Scratch and Dent are examples of discount food markets known for their lower everyday prices. Countless other super-discounted, no-frills grocery outlets and stores are available all over the country in small cities as well as large. Get out there and look. Make it your business to learn everything you can about the no-frills stores in your community. Learn the ropes; ask the right questions. Some of these stores will have everything you need, all at lower prices. Others will concentrate on just nonperishables.

Discount Warehouse Clubs

If you do all of your food shopping at Costco, Sam's Club, or BJ's, you will spend a lot of money. It is difficult, if not impossible, to consistently slash your food costs at these big box stores. You will, however, come home with greater quantities of high-quality foods, meats, and name-brand items. If you have the personal discipline to be selective and you possess industrial-strength restraint, you can make excellent buys.

You can always count on these items to be cheaper at one of the clubs than at a typical supermarket, even when on sale: milk, cheese, eggs, butter, frozen chicken breasts, and laundry detergent.

ALDI

This discount grocery chain operates over seven hundred stores in twenty-six states, primarily from Kansas to the East Coast (see Aldi.com for store locator). ALDI carries only private-label foods and boasts that it prices everything 50 percent less than its competitors.

Most customers find they can do 90 percent of their weekly shopping at ALDI. When you shop at ALDI, you don't worry about coupons, sales, or other marketing ploys. It's a true no-frills operation—expect to put a quarter into the slot to "rent" a shopping cart (you'll get it back when you leave) and also to pay a small fee for grocery bags. Of course, you can bring your own bags. ALDI encourages recycling.

WALMART

All Walmart stores have food departments. A supercenter combines a typical Walmart store with a full-service super-market. Those who are familiar with these stores report that the savings are impressive. Walmart accepts manufacturer's coupons but does not double them.

The unique feature of Walmart is the price match. This policy prevents you from having to drive to many stores to pick up the lowest-priced sale items. Provided you have the competition's weekly ad with you at the checkout to verify the competing price, Walmart will give you the lower price. As a wise shopper, be sure to check on the way this policy is handled at your local store to avoid a time-consuming snag at the checkout.

GREEN MARKETS

While we normally think of produce, green markets also offer other items like bakery goods, meat, and so forth. This is an opportunity to buy directly from the grower, maker, butcher, or baker. The appeal? No middleman.

You should find prices at a green market lower than at the supermarket, and these prices are generally negotiable. Simply ask, "Is this your best price?" Shopping at a green market may be a way to reduce your food costs, but be careful. It's easy to overspend because the bargains at a green market can be so enticing.

BAKERY OUTLETS

Most cities have an outlet store where the overstock from a commercial bakery is sold at bargain-basement prices. While you might think such a place would be well known and in a location you cannot miss, this is not always the case. You need to ask around or look it up online.

While the prices at such an outlet are already amazingly low (remember, they need to get rid of this stuff quickly to make room for tomorrow's overruns), to get even better deals, shop on the day when everything is marked down even further. This makes it possible to buy bread and other bakery items for just pennies on the dollar.

A simple search for "bakery outlets" should turn up local, independent bakeries that have an outlet store or simply reduce prices at the end of the day.

Organic and Natural Foods

If you are committed to a diet of organic foods, you know that decision can be expensive. Still, if you are as committed to reducing the cost as you are to keeping true to an organic way of life, you can accomplish both for a reduced price.

The most expensive way to purchase organic foods is at a high-priced store like Whole Foods. If you must shop at such a store, apply the principles of reserve shopping to buy only what's on sale at the expensive organic store, then do your needs shopping elsewhere.

Your Own Garden

The only way you can be 100 percent sure of what goes into your produce is to grow it yourself. If you require organic foods and you are not supporting a garden, you are allowing a lot of money to leak out of your life. It does not take a great deal of space to grow basic vegetables and herbs. You can do it in containers on a balcony, or you can grow fresh herbs year-round on a windowsill.

Farmer's Markets

Produce is typically cheaper and fresher at a farmer's market. If you don't see a sign saying the produce is organic, ask. Many farmers are making the transition to organic farming. The key to making good deals at these kinds of markets is to ask lots of questions. Ask the farmer about seconds (produce that isn't perfect) that may be available at a discount. A simple "Are you discounting any subprime produce today?" is an easy way to find out what kind of bargains are waiting for you.

COMMUNITY GARDENS

If you do not have space at your home for a garden, you may be able to join a community garden where you rent a plot of ground. If eating organic produce is important to you, making the time and effort in this way will save you a ton of money. Ask if there is a community garden in your area or perhaps help start one. Often there are people with land lying dormant who are happy to let a group farm it free of charge. In a community garden, everyone contributes and divides the harvest.

COMMUNITY-SUPPORTED AGRICULTURE (CSA)

In a CSA, consumers and farmers work together to produce organic produce. While the farmer tends the crops, consumers share the costs of supporting the farm and share the risk of variable harvests (and also share the overabundance of a particularly fruitful year). Membership in a CSA is based on shares of the harvest. Members are called shareholders and underwrite the harvest for the entire season in advance.

A share in a CSA costs about $300 to $400 for a twenty-four- to twenty-six-week growing season. Many programs accept monthly payments. Most CSAs allow singles or small families to buy a half share. To find a CSA in your area, go to www.nal.usda.gov/afsic/pubs/csa/csa.shtml and click on "Find a CSA Farm."

GROCERY CO-OPS

A co-op will be much cheaper than a supermarket like Whole Foods, but don't expect it to be fancy. In fact, your co-op may be housed in a warehouse or a garage. Foods are usually sold in bulk, and co-op members are often asked to volunteer time to run the co-op.

Buying food is the best and easiest place for you to begin living your life for half the price. Yes, this will require some amount of toil and trouble, but the payoff will be more than worth your effort. Just make sure you set a spending limit before you clip a single coupon or print a weekly shopping list.

And one more thing. Clear a space for your stockpile. If I've convinced you to become a reserve shopper, you're going to need it!

5

News Flash! There's a Kitchen in Your House

Dinner in half an hour? Even if you're working all day, why buy Chinese take-out food, or frozen dinners, or eat at a fast food joint when you can make a fresh, informal home-cooked meal even in a minuscule kitchen — and you will know exactly what you are eating.

Julia Child, chef and TV host, *The Way to Cook*

Having a well-stocked pantry, freezer, and refrigerator is fabulous. But alas, acquiring the food is only half the job. It takes commitment to turn that food into quick, easy, and delicious meals so you stay out of the drive-thru.

Your success in buying groceries for half the price will be for naught unless you follow through by turning that food into home-cooked meals instead of eating out. This is critical because failure to exercise the discipline required to eat your meals from your stockpile of groceries will result in paying twice—once for the groceries and then again to eat out because you're too tired or simply cannot be bothered spending time in that area of your home known as the kitchen.

I want to motivate and inspire you to fix family-friendly fare in less time than it takes to have pizza delivered. Or the time it takes to find your keys, drive to a take-out restaurant, wait in line, drive forward to the menu board, decide what you want, place your order, pay at the first window, wait for your order at the second window, drive home hoping nothing spills, carry all of it into the house, and finally look in the bag to discover half your order is missing. Don't you hate it when that happens?

If there's only one thing you take from this chapter, let it be this: You do not have to be a seasoned home chef to create tasty meals in thirty minutes or less. You don't even have to be a good cook. If you can open packages, use a measuring cup, lift the lid from a slow cooker, slide a chicken into the oven, and boil a pan of water, you have what it takes to get started.

No matter where you fall in the demographic spectrum—a single guy in a big-city apartment with a kitchen the size of a postage stamp, the mom of a big, busy family with a kitchen to match, or any of the many possibilities in between—I have confidence that you can turn out quick-and-easy meals for a lot less than you currently spend on food.

I'm assuming that you've begun grocery shopping in keeping with the principles and instructions in the previous chapter. As such, I know what will be making up your stockpile.

The same things go on sale like clockwork. But before we go over what you can expect to find in your stockpile, let's talk about that place known to many of us as the "State of Overwhelmed." That is where you can easily find yourself if you take stockpiling seriously. But, please, do not despair! Do not leave me now! I promise not to leave you overwhelmed.

Because I can't leave you now and come back in a few months once you've gone through the gradual process of building a reserve of food, I need to approach this as if you have your reserve established. And while you won't find recipes in this chapter, I couldn't help myself. I had to make sure you would have access to a handy supply of my can't-live-without recipes and instructions for how to turn a food reserve into fabulous meals that will keep you and your family eating at home. You will find these in appendix A.

So take a deep breath . . . and let's move on with an overview of the foods you'll see a lot of in the coming months.

The Staples

Chicken

You need a good chicken repertoire because once you begin to diligently buy mainly what's on sale, you'll be eating a lot of chicken. You'll have whole chickens as well as boneless chicken breasts, cut-up fryers, wings, thighs, and drumsticks. All of it is good for your health and your spending plan.

Rice

Not only is rice cheap, but it is also a healthy and delicious side dish for almost any meat entree. You need to know the tricks to making perfect rice quickly and efficiently. Decide now to add brown rice to your diet and your repertoire. It is healthier and extraordinarily delicious when prepared properly. Just keep in mind that white rice cooks more rapidly than brown and is always an excellent side dish.

Beef

Once you get into the swing of things, you will find yourself buying lots of London broil or other cheaper cuts of beef because often they will be on sale at bargain prices. You need a variety of ways to prepare these so they come out tender and flavorful. That's a challenge because cheaper cuts of meat can easily turn out tough and bland.

Pasta

When eaten in moderation, pasta is an important part of a well-rounded, nutritious diet. And believe me when I say you will have lots of pasta in your grocery cart once you begin buying what's on sale. When pasta is on sale and you have a coupon to match, it is an almost-free pantry item. You need many options for using pasta in your homemade meals.

Legumes

Otherwise known as beans, legumes should find a place in your regular meal lineup. I suggest that one meal each week should have legumes as the entree. Pinto beans, lima beans, black-eyed peas, lentils, and navy beans are always cheap. And while legumes may never make the list of sensational sale items the way cold cereal and salad dressings do, they are always a bargain—even when you pay the full retail price. And when they are on sale, load up.

Ground Beef

You'll find ground beef on sale often. Sometimes it will be the leanest variety, but quite often not. Regardless, you should buy ground beef when the price is right. Then you need to know how to quickly and efficiently get that ground beef cooked and virtually fat-free. It's easy, as you will learn when you cruise through appendix A. Cooked ground beef is a basic staple item you should freeze so it's available at a minute's notice.

Freezer-Ready Food

This is what I call anything like ground beef, rice, sliced turkey, chicken stock, beef broth, lasagna, and homemade cookies, all of which I've prepared partway then frozen in portion sizes for future use. If you could peek into my freezer right now, you'd see about twenty zip-type bags, each containing about one pound of browned ground beef or cooked rice in individual-portion sizes; two pans of homemade lasagna; dozens of one-cup portions of homemade chicken stock; and ditto on the beef broth. It is so quick and easy for me to put together a meal in no time flat from this collection of meal ingredients.

Cake Mixes

Cake mixes go on sale often. When they are priced at their lowest, you can get cake mixes for a couple of bucks or less. Knowing what to do with a cake mix other than following the package instructions will bring great variety to your meals, because you'll have quick-and-easy desserts on the menu.

You can make cookies from cake mix or use a cake mix as a quick-and-easy base for a more elaborate dessert that tastes and looks like you made it from scratch (my favorite way to cook, sometimes called "semi-homemade").

Produce

Is it possible to eat a healthy diet on a tight budget? The answer is yes. Still, many believe that a cheap diet is one loaded with carbohydrates, lacking in the fruits and vegetables that we know are necessary in a healthy diet.

The Department of Agriculture put this question to rest with publication of the study "How Much Do Americans Pay for Fruits and Vegetables?"[1] Americans can meet fruit-and-vegetable food pyramid recommendations for as little as 64 cents a day. The same report found 127 ways to eat a serving of fruits and vegetables for less than the price of a 3-ounce candy bar. Even when adjusting for inflation since this study was conducted,[2] there is very good reason to believe that it is not cost prohibitive to eat a healthy amount of fresh produce. The secret is to buy what's in season.

If you depend on a grocery list service like the Grocery Game or Coupon Mom (see chap. 4), expect to see a variety of fruits and vegetables on those lists each week, year-round. The healthy-diet-conscious shopper will zero in on these items on the list and stock up. If you don't depend on such a list, you can rely on the fact that most grocery stores have a variety of fruits and vegetables on sale each week. The big three in the fresh produce department will be apples, oranges, and grapes—they are on sale most often, but not all the time. This means you will need to change your thinking away from shopping for the familiar standbys to trying new things when the price is right.

The fresh produce department is not the only place to find fruits and vegetables. You will find items that meet the standards in the canned, frozen, and dried fruits aisles of the supermarket too. Let the sales be your guide.

Have you ever wondered what constitutes "a serving" in the context of the daily recommendations from the US Department of Agriculture? It is likely less than you might think. A small apple, for example, is considered one serving. But a large apple counts as two servings.

The National Cancer Institute, cosponsor of the 5 A Day for Better Health program, defines a serving as:

- 4 ounces of applesauce (any variety or brand)
- 1 medium-sized piece of fruit (or 4 ounces by weight)
- ½ cup raw, cooked, frozen, or canned fruit (in 100 percent juice)
- ½ cup raw, cooked, frozen, or canned vegetable
- ¾ cup (6 ounce) 100 percent fruit or vegetable juice
- ½ cup cooked, frozen, or canned legumes (beans and peas)
- 1 cup raw, leafy vegetables
- ⅛ cup raisins
- ¼ cup other dried fruit[3]

Getting five or more servings of fruits and vegetables into your diet every day is easier than you think. It's also much more likely now that you have taken control of your grocery shopping and committed to eating most of your meals from that food.

A glass of 100 percent juice and a handful of berries on your cereal equals two servings for breakfast. An apple or banana is a great one-serving mid-morning snack. A small, mixed-green salad adds another serving with lunch. Try a fruit smoothie as an afternoon pick-me-up for one to two more servings.

Mushrooms in your stir-fry? Tomato sauce on your spaghetti? A snack of dried fruits and nuts? There are so many ways to add more servings of fruits and vegetables to your daily diet.

Specials of the House

You need a repertoire of simple dishes, six to eight entrees or meals you can make with speed and confidence that you and your family enjoy. You may already have such a list. If not, here are some ideas to help you get started (you will find specific recipes and directions for some of these and others in appendix A). Just make sure you keep it simple or you'll not likely stick with it.

Spaghetti is always a family-pleasing entree, so learn to make it. You'll need a couple of good, reliable entrees that use ground beef, such as chili or meat sauce (for spaghetti or a host of other uses). You need to know how to make a great stir-fry from ingredients you have on hand (even leftovers) and a great casserole (you're going to love the ideas in appendix A for "designer cuisine"). Homemade pizza has every hope of becoming your number-one favorite quick-and-easy home-cooked meal.

Once you discover the meals you enjoy, claim them as your specialties of the house. Fix them on a regular basis. Yes, over and over again. Aren't you and your family eating the same fast food over and over? The same principles apply with the great food you fix at home for half the price and in half the time. Your family will beg you not to eat out again once they realize what a great cook you are—and fast too. Well, perhaps "beg" is a bit strong, but you get my point.

Return of the Slow Cooker

The slow cooker (known to many by the brand name Crock-Pot, though there are other brands) is back, and in a big way. If you have a slow cooker packed away, now would be a great time to drag it out and give it another chance.

I know what you're thinking. The reason that slow cooker landed where it did is because it produced overcooked and bland meals that could, at best, be considered semi-edible. I hear you. The problem is we probably didn't know (much less follow) the basic fundamental culinary techniques of slow cooking. But that was then, now is now, and a slow cooker may well become your culinary lifesaver.

One of the best things about slow cooking is that it requires some level of planning ahead. It does cook very slowly, after all. Loading the cooker in the morning guarantees a more stress-free afternoon and evening because you've already done the minimum amount of work required. And as a bonus, you'll have a delicious meal waiting when everyone returns home that day. You will bless the day you took my advice to call this wonderful appliance back into service.

Why Slow Cook?

Convenience. A slow cooker can be left unattended all day. You can put in ingredients in the morning and forget about it until dinnertime without worrying it will burn your house down. It's as safe as a night-light.

Economy. The best slow-cooked ingredients are often the least expensive (tough cuts of beef, the dark part of the chicken, root vegetables). Knowing dinner is all ready to go prevents·unscheduled fast-food runs and relieves guilt. The folks at Sunbeam say it costs only a penny to operate a slow cooker for six to eight hours. How awesome is that?

Basic Guidelines

Know sizes and styles. Popular sizes are 3½-, 4-, and 5-quart models. Most have removable liners. The 3½-quart models are fine for most dishes and needs, but the 5-quart models allow you to insert other dishes, springform pans, or pudding molds, giving you a wider range of options.

Rival's Crock-Pot models, Smart-Pots, have fancy timers; some are programmable and allow you to set the time and temperature to cook in thirty-minute increments for up to twenty intervals, or ten hours. As interesting as all that might sound, you don't need anything that fancy to get started with slow cooking.

Manufacturers usually recommend filling the pot half to three-quarters full, so if you're cooking for two, this might be an important consideration. The secret to successful slow cooking is to use the right size cooker. You can still get a good slow cooker for less than $50. Watch for sales at stores like Target or Walmart. Go to Google Shopping and type in "slow cooker" to see the vast array of choices.

Know your cooker. A traditional slow cooker where the heat surrounds the cooking insert is better than a slow cooker where the heat comes from underneath. All models available these days have a removable pot insert. The two heat settings are low (200 degrees) and high (300 degrees).

Find slow cooker recipes. Until you become slow cooker proficient, stick closely to a recipe that has been specifically developed for slow cooking. Go to the food and beverage area of About.com where you will find thousands of recipes for slow cooking and everything you ever wanted to know about the technique. Bookmark that site because you will use it frequently.

Rival's Crock-Pot website (CrockPot.com) has a nice collection of slow-cooking recipes. Another favorite source of recipes for slow cooking is Crockery Kitchen (CrockPot.cd-kitchen.com). There are many cookbooks in print for slow cooking and tons of free ones online.

Master the Stir-Fry

If you want to learn to do something impressive in the kitchen, this is it. Who doesn't love a good stir-fry? The reason I love it: no recipe, just technique. If your family is anti-leftovers, do not tell them this part: It's the perfect way to clean out the refrigerator. You need some of this and a little of that.

The reason most home stir-fry comes out a soggy mess is that our home stovetops don't get as hot as restaurant woks. The secret is to cook everything very quickly on high heat and in small batches. Then remove those small batches from the skillet or wok until the end, when you put all the cooked batches back into the same pot and toss with a great sauce.

I have such confidence in you that I'm going to make this bold statement: You can make stir-fry start to finish in fewer than thirty minutes. The secret is to get all your ingredients ready and within easy reach before you start and to get your skillet as hot as possible.

You will find my favorite instructions (and recipes for the sauce too) in appendix A, together with some of my favorite shortcuts and kitchen helps. Enjoy!

You Deserve Some Help

Allrecipes.com

The internet has untold sites filled with recipes, so many, in fact, that you could find yourself paralyzed and unable to cook a meal for all of the information available. So in an act of mercy, I offer my single most favorite recipe website, Allrecipes.com. At this site, you can search by the ingredients you have on hand, by recipe title, or by recipe collection, such as their "Quick and Easy" collection.

The most helpful feature on this site, in my opinion, is the reviews by others who have tested the recipes. I feel as if I've been to cooking school after reading comments and suggestions. It gives me confidence to try new things, improve my recipes, or make the same strategic changes to recipes as reviewers describe.

Cookbooks

I hesitate even to bring this up. The typical kitchen has at least seventeen cookbooks already, most of them doubling as colorful dust collectors. However, I find several cookbooks invaluable. Before buying them, however, see if you can find them at the library. Take them home for a couple of weeks and see how they work for you.

Desperation Dinners! by Beverly Mills and Alicia Ross (Workman, 1997; DesperationDinners.com). Written by two working moms with four kids between them, this friendly cookbook fulfills its promise to supply families with more than 250 recipes that can be made from start to finish in twenty minutes.

The Rush-Hour Cook's Weekly Wonders by Brook Noel (Champion Press, 2003). Part of a series of Rush Hour Cook publications, this book presents nineteen weekly dinner menus complete with grocery lists for today's busy families. ,

Quick & Healthy Low-Fat, Carb-Conscious Cooking by Brenda Ponichtera, RD (ScaleDown Publishing, Inc., 2005). This cookbook offers help for people who say they don't have time to cook healthy meals.

eMeals

You know you should stick to buying what's on sale each week. But for many, that presents a bigger problem than it's meant to solve! What are you supposed to do with all of this seemingly unrelated sale bounty? Sure, it was cheap, but it's no bargain if you don't use it.

An online service, eMeals, offers a solution that may be right for you. Each week, a team of clever moms creates dinner menus from the food items that will be on sale in your supermarket that week. Once each week, members receive an email with a menu plan for six dinners, the recipes and instructions to make the meals, and a grocery shopping list to go with it. The shopping list is in aisle order for the store layout and includes the sale prices (expect to spend about $75 at the grocery store for the sale items required to feed a family of four to six).

If you are just too busy and frazzled to wade through the store's weekly ad, buy what's on sale, and then find recipes for the coming week that use those ingredients—eMeals is eager to come to your rescue.

Currently, eMeals offers specific plans for four supermarket chains: Winn-Dixie (Thrift Way), Publix, Walmart Super-center, and some Kroger stores. In addition, it offers an "any store" low-carb plan. A $5 monthly fee allows you to print your menus and shopping list from the site. Visit eMeals.com for more information.

5 Dollar Dinners

I saved the best for last. Erin Chase, founder of 5 Dollar Dinners, admits that she has a problem. She cannot make a meal that costs more than $5. And I'm not talking five bucks per person but $5 for a meal that feeds four or five people.

Erin founded her website 5dollardinners.com years ago. Since then, food prices have skyrocketed. Still, she turns out recipes, directions, how-tos, shopping lists, coupon lists, and every manner of help imaginable. And she does it with ex-cellence. Her recipes, meal plans, and menus continue to be fabulous. So check it out and prepare to be amazed. Your family will be so happy, and so will your budget. And did I mention that 5dollardinners.com is free? It is!

6

The Mother of All
Budget Busters

I've been so busy, I don't even have time to cook
for my kids. I don't want to say we eat out a lot,
but I've noticed lately when I call them for dinner
they run to the car.

Julie Kidd, comedian

For most people, eating out is such a normal and acceptable part of daily living that it is like breathing. They go in and out, hardly aware of what they are doing. Unfortunately, for many, it's like breathing polluted air for all the damage it is doing to their finances. As minor as eating out may seem, it is likely one of the biggest drains on your disposable income. It just might be an area of spending ripe for serious reduction without sacrificing the life you love.

Here's the problem in a nutshell: Ready-to-eat food and drinks are so available that it's a no-brainer—literally. You don't even have to think about it. It takes more brain power and effort to get dinner on the table than to stop for take-out on the way home from work. Packing a lunch at home takes more time and effort than grabbing something on the run.

My definition of "eating out" is paying for food prepared by others instead of eating meals you make from the groceries you buy. That makes eating out a very broad category because it refers to donut shops, lunches purchased at work and school, coffee breaks, trips to the vending machine, fast food, diners, and cafes. It includes picking up takeout, having pizza delivered, eating multiple-course meals in fancy restaurants, and everything in between.

To get a handle on this runaway expense, it is best that we divide eating out into two categories: meal replacements and entertainment.

Meal replacements are necessary at those times when for one reason or another you are not at home and cannot get to your food at home. It's meal time and you gotta eat!

Eating out for the pure joy of it may contribute to the quality of your life. If so, that should be seen as a form of entertainment. But for now it is essential to see eating out as two separate activities—one to be avoided whenever possible and the other to be treated as one of the good things in life, so plan accordingly.

Nothing will sabotage your efforts to slash your grocery bill and drain your finances faster than unnecessary meal replacements. You can corral this area by making a commitment to eat as many of your meals as humanly possible at home from the groceries you purchase.

Meal Replacements

You can't predict the unpredictable, but when it comes to replacing meals, you can come close. Simply becoming aware of how much you and your family members eat out and how much it costs you should help tame this runaway expense. And then when it cannot be avoided, make sure you at out as inexpensively as possible. After all, wouldn't you rather spend your eating-out dollars on a planned meal you count as entertainment than let so much money leak out of your life through a meaningless "gulp and go" replacement meal?

Unless you live in a remote area or are extremely disciplined, it is likely you won't banish all meal replacements from your life. After you've identified which eating-out activities count as entertainment, what's left should be considered meal replacements. Your goal is this: When you can't ban, plan! You want to eliminate as many meal replacements as possible and then plan ahead for those you cannot avoid.

Here's an example of how to logically plan for simple meal replacements. Let's say you have a $3.50-a-day latte routine. You hardly consider this entertainment—but you don't want to give up your coffee either. What you may not be aware of is the significant drain this places on your income.

You need to make an allowance for this by planning ahead. Here are your choices:

1. Once each month put $75 cash into an envelope to allow for this daily excursion into Latte Land. Didn't know it would be that much? It gets even better. At a rate of five lattes a week, you will spend $910 in a year's time. Or . . .

2. Switch from a latte to a large coffee of the day (typically half the cost at most coffee bars), step to the side, and pour in your own creamer from the supplies provided at no additional cost. Remarkably, it tastes about the same. This reduces your morning coffee expense to about $38.50 a month, freeing up $455 in a year's time. Or . . .

3. Invest in a coffeemaker with a timer. Once a month, purchase quality coffee beans along with your groceries. The cost of coffee and milk (to replicate the lattes) will run about $22, or about half of option 2. Annual recoup? Another $225. Or . . .

4. Invest a little toil and trouble in the effort to roast your own coffee beans (one of my personal favorite hobbies, something I explain in appendix B). Now you will spend about $10 a month, have better-tasting coffee than you will find at any coffee bar in town, pick up a new hobby, and reclaim an additional $225 of your hard-earned money each year. Spend $10 every couple of months to purchase sturdy disposable cups with lids at a restaurant supply or discount warehouse club or reuse your own travel mug and keep the change.

This is intended to demonstrate how the simple task of analyzing and planning your meal replacements can reduce the cost or eliminate the replacement altogether.

Lunch at Work

Here's another common meal replacement situation. You eat lunch out every day because you work and that's just what you prefer to do. Okay. What's the tab? About $10 a day? Sounds low to me, but that's fine. Just make sure you are planning ahead with $50 cash in an envelope each week earmarked for work lunches. And it's $3 more for coffee breaks each day? Better add another $15 to the envelope—that's $65 a week.

By my calculations, if you work fifty weeks a year, that's $3,250 that go toward replacing one meal and providing a snack or beverage at break time each day for one person in the family. I'm not saying this is wrong or that you shouldn't do it. I am only holding up a mirror and a light for you to see for yourself the high cost of meal replacements.

What options do you have? As elementary as it may seem, preparing a meal at home and bringing it with you is an option. It takes time and a modicum of planning. You have to decide if the financial result is worth the toil and trouble.

Instead of going cold turkey (pun intended) all five days, start by bringing your lunch two or three days a week. Calculating the savings is likely to encourage you to put forth the effort or at the very least to give it a try. Multiplying this effort times the number of people in the household who pay for lunch meal replacements could add up to some serious money over a year's time.

The Challenges of a Busy Lifestyle

I am not privy to all of the challenges you face that prompt meal replacements. But let's say that Tuesday is your kids' soccer practice day. By the time you drive carpool, there is no time to go home for dinner before getting the kids to the field.

Logistically, you have to eat out. That's fine. Just plan now to put $35 into an envelope each week for that excursion into Fast-Food Land. And while we're talking about kids and school, there are school lunches, ice-cream treats, sodas, pizza, fries, and an occasional snack from the corner store. What do you think? Another $40 a week? Okay, set it aside. In cash. In a trusty envelope.

It All Adds Up

Start adding up all the known meal replacements you will face over a week's time (or a month if you are brave). That's a lot of dough. You can't ignore it and hope it will go away. Either you plan ahead and have the cash to pay, or you depend on plastic to pay for meal replacements.

Unfortunately, now most fast-food places allow you to swipe any kind of plastic you happen to have handy. It is dreadful to think that some people add the cost of burgers and fries to an already out-of-control credit card balance. Maybe that's you.

What if you could move away from meal replacements altogether by planning ahead, packing lunches, making coffee at home, arranging things so you bring food with you from home on soccer practice night, and so forth? Now you are eating from the food you purchased at the grocery store. You are preparing meals from your stockpile.

Much of the money you spend on meal replacements could be channeled elsewhere. You do not have unlimited sources of money, and it is a shame to think of how much of what you have simply leaks out of your life in meaningless meal replacements. Perhaps that's the money you need to build an emergency fund or to pay off your debts. At the very least, those funds could be moved to your entertainment fund so you could actually take joy in eating out rather than allowing that money to vanish into thin air with nothing to show for it.

I received a letter from a reader who explained that she and her mother live together and enjoy eating at a national chain. As a regular routine, they stop in for a simple breakfast and coffee, nothing elaborate. In their minds, this was quite a benign activity. That is until they took me up on my challenge to track their spending for a month. With an amazing degree of shock, they told me that in one month they spent more than $385 at that chain. That works out to an average of $12.83 a day.

Can you imagine how much the typical family spends on fast food in a month? How about your family? Don't imagine anymore. Do the work to find out.

While your goal is to eliminate meal replacements, getting to that point may take some time. But you can start now. Wean yourself from your drive-thru habit. When you have food at home and plan ahead to prepare that food, you won't have the continual need to eat out, which will be your saving grace. You won't have a nagging sense that you have nothing to eat at home and no time to run to the market.

From now on when you eat a replacement meal because you have no choice (dubious), see that money as coming out of your grocery allotment for the week or month. It won't take long to begin thinking differently about that pathetic-looking salad or skimpy burger. You'll find yourself saying, "I can make this at home for so much less, and it will taste a lot better too." And when that meal replacement tab comes to $20, $25, or more, you will see it in terms of how many groceries that same amount of money could have purchased.

If you are successful in eliminating meal replacements altogether, good for you. If not, it's important you replace meals as economically as possible.

How to Save Money on Meal Replacements

Plan ahead. Let's say it's Tuesday again, the day your kids have soccer practice. Despite your best efforts to get dinner on the table in plenty of time to make practice or to bring food with you from home, something came up. You must feed the kids on the run to make it to practice on time. To pop into the first place you see for a round of burgers, fries, and drinks could prove very expensive. A better option: hit the taco joint down the street because it's Taco Tuesday! You can get a bag of ten tacos for $5— a bargain in any book.

While you hope to replace meals rarely, it's good to have a survival plan. Find out where the Taco Tuesdays are in your town. Look through the paper and mailers for coupons. Fast-food chains often have midweek family specials, typically on Tuesday, the day that supermarkets and restaurants see the fewest customers. Know what they are so you can make a good decision when the need arises.

Use discounts. Many restaurants offer a reduced-price menu for seniors and children. If you or someone in your party qualifies, be sure to inquire if this doesn't show up on the regular menu. Typically, these discounted menus offer smaller portions at significantly reduced prices.

Order down. It never hurts in a regular restaurant to ask if older children or even adults can order from the kids menu. Fast-food restaurants are not likely to have age restrictions, which makes a kids meal an excellent alternative for any age.

Share. Splitting a meal these days is socially acceptable and economically savvy. While some restaurants charge a minimal fee for splitting, most are accommodating. Even if you have to pay a dollar or two to split, it's still better than paying for two meals you cannot eat completely.

If you're embarrassed about sharing, don't be. Many restaurants are so accommodating that they'll split the meal in the kitchen and bring it on two plates. Just don't shortchange your waitperson when it comes time to tip. He or she served two people even if you split the meal.

Order specials. Many restaurants have daily specials priced below their menu price. Be sure to ask about any specials if the server does not volunteer them. Don't want the entire dinner or lunch? Ask for just the entree a la carte.

Be an early bird. Many restaurants, in an effort to build business during their quiet hours, offer half-off meals or some other enticingly priced deal, but only if you're there before the regular dinner crowd, typically from 4:00 to 5:30 p.m. Look in your local newspaper and your mailbox for advertisements and information.

Skip the sodas. Skip the pricey drinks and dubious free refills altogether and you'll save at least $2.50 per person. One of my readers rewards herself whenever she opts for water by stuffing two bucks into her savings account. One mom wrote saying she pays her kids $1 to order water. Not only does that save money, but it also gives the children an incentive to break the soda habit. Everyone's happy.

Order appetizers. Before you opt for a full meal, check the appetizer menu. You'll find generous portions minus the add-ons like salad or soup. And the price is right.

Use coupons. Call the high school to find out who is selling local restaurant discount books or discount cards. Or go to Entertainment.com to find a book of coupons specific to your area. But exercise extreme caution. By the time you adhere to all of the conditions some restaurants impose and tip the waiter as if you had paid full price for the discounted meal, you could end up paying more than you would have had you not used a coupon.

Play tourist. It's not unusual for restaurants to have special offers directed at tourists. Local residents can avail themselves of these offers too, if they can find out about them. Stop by the lobby of a local hotel and peruse the local attractions brochures. Or Google the name of your city or area plus the word *tourist.* You'll find all kinds of offers for local restaurants. Your local tourism board and chamber of commerce will have this kind of information as well.

Order from the lunch menu. Many restaurants have a lunch menu that is slightly different from the one for dinner, the difference being the portion sizes and prices. Ask to order from the lunch menu.

Strategize. Many fast-food chains are competing with each other and trying to drive business with their dollar menus. Some also offer a value upgrade to their already substantial meals, resulting in increased portion sizes. You can use both ends of the spectrum to your advantage. Get creative. Do some figuring ahead of time so you know which combination of items at several fast-food chains makes for the cheapest meal replacements for you or your family.

Here's how one family of four eats at McDonald's for $11. Their secret? No Happy Meals. For the kids (ages three and five), they order one two-cheeseburger value meal (about $4.89). Dad gets a value meal ($4.89). Mom gets a dollar sandwich and shares the fries from the other meals. They still have food left over. It's all about strategy and having a plan before you go.

Check websites. All of the quick-serve chain restaurants have websites with details about their menus. You won't find prices and specials, but cost is not the only factor. Nutrition needs to be of utmost importance. Visiting a few of these websites (McDonald's, Burger King, Jack in the Box, and so on) and clicking on their nutritional lists will be enlightening. It's possible to consume in a single meal an entire week's worth of fat as dictated by any reasonable eating plan. Learn which menu items are low in fat or carbs and so on.

Utilize semi–fast food. Semi–fast food is combining quick-service food with home cooking. Here's an example. The take-out pizza store in my neighborhood sells ready-to-roll pizza dough. I can buy a large ball of dough that makes a sixteen-inch pizza for $2.75. That's slightly more than it costs to make dough from scratch. But when time is of the essence, this is a fast, cheap, high-quality alternative. Using my own sauce and toppings, I can have really great pizza on the table in no time at all. I do rely on this option quite often, particularly when we have last-minute guests. It is impressive to turn out such a high-quality, delicious pizza so quickly. It is my little secret.

Not all pizza stores sell their dough (the national chains in my area look at me as if I have three eyes when I inquire), but independents are typically more than happy for the business—any business. In fact, one store near me even lists this on its menu. Find a pizza place nearby that sells raw dough so you'll know what to do when you're in a bind. You can even freeze the dough and use it to make breadsticks and calzones too.

Just because you don't have an entree for dinner doesn't mean you have to replace the entire meal. You can supplement a big bucket of chicken at home with your own salad and bread. Or maybe you have the chicken but no sides. A large order of coleslaw, corn, and fresh biscuits from the drive-thru will turn that into a complete meal for far less money than buying the entire meal.

As easy as it is to make at home, it pains me to suggest buying rice at a restaurant. But this is a great solution that can reduce an otherwise expensive meal replacement. All Asian restaurants, even the quick-service variety, offer plain white rice as a menu option—usually dirt cheap. I can pick up a large container of white rice for $3 or $4 in my neighborhood. It's hot, fluffy, and perfectly cooked. At home I can serve it plain or enhance it by adding scrambled eggs, soy sauce, leftover chicken, peas, carrots, and so on.

The fanciest fish restaurant in my community has a pricey menu, I mean take-your-breath-away expensive to the point that getting the check all but ruins an otherwise fabulous meal. However, their to-die-for New England clam chowder is renowned and available for takeout at a reasonable price. I can only imagine they are trying to discourage the annoying customers who come in on a cold winter night, take up space at a lovely linen-covered table, and linger over big steaming bowls of hearty chowder, turning down the complete meals and dessert.

That's fine with me because picking up a quart of steaming hot chowder and sourdough rolls (also their specialty) is a terrific way to avoid a huge restaurant tab. Lots of restaurants serve homemade soups that are available for takeout. Check around and then put that on your list of options when you need to fill out or replace a meal inexpensively.

Finally, pizza restaurants are notorious for offering big salads. It might be called a large antipasto salad. Typically, it's a big bed of lettuce and other greens plus a variety of pizza toppings such as onions, olives, peppers, tomatoes, pepperoni, and cheese. Fantastico! Toss it at home with your favorite dressing and you have a large, satisfying, family-sized salad at a side-dish price. In fact, you could make the salad the dinner entree by adding your own ingredients at home, such as hard-cooked eggs, garbanzo beans (chickpeas), leftover chicken, beef, and so on.

Now is the time to start planning how to replace a regular meal more economically. You're smart, so I am confident you will come up with ideas and strategies I've not considered. But don't get too excited. You want meal replacements to be as rare as possible. Otherwise all of the money you are not spending on groceries will get sucked into the big black hole of fast food while the food you buy at the grocery store goes to waste.

Eating Out as Entertainment

Entertainment dollars can be eaten up in a hurry with restaurant meals. But there are ways to stretch your eating-out budget so that you can enjoy—not eliminate—this important entertainment factor. Like all areas of living your life for half the price, you need a plan and the discipline to stick with it.

Go to Self-Serve Restaurants

You can drop 15 to 20 percent (the cost of a tip) from your eating-out tab just by serving yourselves in a restaurant that offers this type of service. Pizza parlors, buffets, and many steak houses, to name a few, offer this type of dining experience. It may seem minor, but that extra $5 or $10 you don't leave as a tip will add up over time. As for restaurants where you mostly serve yourselves, then a staff person drops by with bread and to refill drinks, a tip is in order. My rule of thumb for a tip in that situation is half of what I would tip a full-service waitperson, 8 to 10 percent.

Purchase Gift Certificates

If you know where to look, you can purchase restaurant gift certificates for a fraction of the face value. Of course, there are conditions, but it's worth your consideration. Restaurant.com acts as a community matchmaker, introducing great restaurants to local people. Not all offers are the same, so it makes sense to peruse the restaurants' offerings in your area. From this site you buy gift certificates for these restaurants at a great discount. For example, a $25 food certificate can cost $10. There are conditions you should read before purchasing. However, these conditions are more than reasonable and certainly not difficult to comply with.

Go Where Kids Eat Free

Many restaurants assign Tuesday as the day that kids eat free when parents purchase a meal. This marketing tactic, if acted upon well, can save you a lot of dough.

No More Back-of-the-Closet Mistakes

Women usually love what they buy, yet hate two-thirds of what is in their closets.

Mignon McLaughlin, *The Neurotic's Notebook*

If the 80–20 rule is correct, we wear 20 percent of the clothes we own while 80 percent is banished to the dark side of our closets. Even if this statistic is way off and it's more like 50/50, that still means we waste a lot of money trying to get it right.

Imagine for a moment that by some stroke of luck you had all the cash you've spent in your wardrobe-buying lifetime on clothes that you didn't wear. That's the kind of money you'll be able to keep in the future, once you learn how to stop making those back-of-the-closet mistakes.

Here's the problem. We shop for clothes with no particular plan in mind. If it fits, it's a definite candidate; if it is also on sale, it's a done deal. But eight purchases out of ten are not right, so they end up in the back of the closet or stuffed into a drawer. That's an expensive approach to wardrobe building.

What, Where, and When

Slashing the cost of a wardrobe is less about bargains and more about knowing what to buy, where to buy, and when to stop buying. The way to cut your clothing costs by half the price is to reduce your wardrobe to the equivalent of the 20 percent you wear now and stop wasting money on back-of-the-closet mistakes.

With this mind-set, not only will you buy clothes in an entirely new way than you have in the past, but you will also recognize when your wardrobe is complete. And you will be willing to stop buying clothes even though unbelievable bargains remain to be had. The ability to stop shopping is critical to your success in dressing well for half the price.

The best wardrobes are built around classic designs and are developed over time, one piece at a time. And they last. This minimalist approach to building a wardrobe makes so much sense—fashion sense and economic sense. When you have twelve to fifteen well-chosen classic and timeless items in your closet that you like, that fit well, and that look good on you, you can create thirty or forty different outfits. Even if all twelve or fifteen items are high-quality designer labels, there's no doubt you will spend far less with this approach than you will buying hundreds of items from sale racks, none of which complement each other or fit very well either.

You Need a Uniform

Your "uniform" is your look, your signature style. Everyone needs to create a personal uniform that addresses his or her taste or style, color palette, and body type. When determining your uniform, incorporate all of these things.

Think about your favorite outfit. I can almost guarantee that it is one of your most flattering colors, it fits you well, and it reflects your taste and style. It's you! Color, style, and fit work together to make it work for you.

It's just a guess, but I'll bet the 80 percent of your wardrobe that you don't wear is all over the map. It's likely those items don't fit right and are the wrong colors and styles for you. Why did you buy those clothes? Let me guess. They were on sale.

Or maybe that dress was really cute. It didn't quite fit, but you figured that would be your incentive to lose ten pounds. And you justified that the color would be passable if you wore the right blush and lipstick. Do you wonder why that dress languishes in the back of your closet, tags still attached, next to so many other completely wrong choices? Those items are not you and never will be you. Even at rock-bottom prices, you're looking at very expensive closet stuffers.

Your uniform is a filter through which every clothing purchase will pass, whether it's a sweater you knit by hand, a designer blazer from the thrift store, or jeans from the department store. Your uniform is your personal fashion safety net that will keep you from being seduced by clothes that are simply not right for you, even if they are fantastic bargains.

Know Your Colors

Each of us has natural coloring that is part of our DNA. It shows up in the color of our hair, eyes, and skin. The premise behind color analysis is that certain colors enhance one's looks and make a person look healthier, radiant, and more alive, whereas other colors will make the person look washed out or sallow. The predominant tone or color just under your skin is what determines if you have blue/red (cool) undertones or yellow/orange (warm) undertones. The colors you wear close to your face should complement these natural tones.

Some department stores offer a color analysis service for a fee. You can also go to StyleMakeovers.com for a simple, free online analysis. Or check your library for the book *Color Me Beautiful* by Carole Jackson (Ballantine Books, 1987). This book, now a classic, has been around for many years and is still relevant.

With a big mirror, good lighting, and a friend to offer a second opinion, you should be able to confidently determine your color palette. Your confidence will grow once you can tell that something is the right color for you and also when something that may fit well is simply not right because it is the wrong color.

Discover Your Personality

If you find yourself always gravitating to the same types and styles of clothes—tailored, feminine, dramatic, sporty—you are simply expressing your clothing personality. Most of us have an inborn tendency to favor a particular style and type of apparel. Whether frilly feminine, sporty natural, simply classic, or head-turning dramatic, that is you. Your clothing personality will give you clues to establish your uniform. Trust your taste.

Living your life for half the price does not mean you deny your style and taste. On the contrary, embracing a specific uniform will help you save money because you will stop buying things that are not you.

Understand the Shape of You

You do not need a model's figure or physique to look great in your clothes. No matter your height, weight, and proportions, if you know what you should wear for your body type, you'll stop wasting your money on clothes that look great on the hanger but are all wrong in the mirror.

Your silhouette—the essential frame you were born with—should always be the number one consideration when making a clothing decision. If a garment is the wrong shape, it will never fit you no matter what size you try on. Your measurements will change as you go through the seasons of life, but your frame is the one part of your clothing equation that will never change. You need to identify your body type, make friends with it just the way it is, and then learn how to dress it to your best advantage.

Once you know your body type, it will be easier to discover the right pant style for you, the best necklines, which skirt length you should wear, what to avoid, and the exact style and cut of jean that will make you feel and look great. It's like slipping a key into a locked door to open a new world of clothing understanding and half-price living.

Several theories and explanations of body types can be found in countless books and on websites. The simplest and my personal favorite is found in *The Pocket Stylist* by Kendall Farr (Gotham, 2004). Clothing is always designed for silhouette first, measurements second, and that is true of all clothing from low end to high, cheap to expensive. An item of clothing that is not cut to your silhouette will never fit your shape—no matter what size it is, no matter how cute it is, no matter that it's your perfect color, and no matter how many times it has been marked down.

A simple way to describe your shape uses letters and a number. If you are an A, you are smaller at the top than the bottom. V is just the opposite. H is straight up and down, while 8 is curvaceous. Some analysts call these body types apple-shaped, pear-shaped, triangle-shaped, and so on. At the risk of destroying any mental images you may have of your humble author, I'll use myself as an example. I am an A. My shoulders slope slightly, and I carry my weight below my waist. There, I said it. My height dictates my need for clothes that are cut and designed for petites (under 5 feet 4 inches is considered petite), because the length of sleeves, jackets, skirts, and pants are shorter in petite sizes than in regular sizes.

Let's talk about pants. I know I should never wear cropped pants because they visually shorten my legs. I need to make my legs appear longer, not cut off at midcalf. Part of my uniform is a pant that is straight all the way to the bottom or flares out a bit. It should be long so that it sits right at the top of my shoes when I'm wearing heels. It's a visual thing. And because I know this, I am not even tempted a tiny bit to buy cropped capri pants—even if they fit, even if they are the right color, and even if they are on sale. That is a fashion risk I'm not willing to take. And on a positive note, that's an entire fashion trend I won't be wasting money on!

I have specific guidelines in my uniform for the necklines best for me (boat neck, ballet neck, square neck, V-necks, and a plethora of other shapes that draw the eye upward). I don't wear bulky textures or large prints. In fact, my uniform pretty much rules out prints altogether. I could go on, but I think you get the point.

Knowing what to buy makes buying the right clothes a lot easier. Knowing my colors, body type, and personal taste is the best insurance against expensive mistakes—clothes that look great on the hanger but I'll never wear because they are so wrong for me.

A Wardrobe Plan

As you can tell by now, I'm into plans. There's just one thing I need to tell you about a wardrobe plan: You need one. This is a plan you design specifically for your lifestyle and uniform. Your wardrobe plan will save you money, frustration, and time.

Building your wardrobe should not be a never-ending endeavor. In fact, it is possible you are well on your way with the clothes you have already. You'll never know without a plan. There comes a time when your wardrobe is complete and you move into maintenance mode. But without a plan, you will not know when that day arrives. Without a plan, you'll just keep spending money, very likely needlessly.

There is no one-size-fits-all wardrobe plan. Your plan depends on your lifestyle. A single career woman in Manhattan who participates in sports on the weekends will have a completely different plan than a stay-at-home mom in Missoula who is involved in community activities. But both need a written plan if they are determined to live below their means.

Basically, a wardrobe plan establishes basic clothing items. Even the most extensive plan is still quite simple compared to the quantity of clothes most people have. Any professional stylist will tell you that the key to making a plan work is for all the pieces in your wardrobe to coordinate in both style and color. Once you have the basic pieces, you can create many looks and many outfits within the framework of the clothes you have.

Below are simple samples of wardrobe plans for career adults (you'll find kids' wardrobe plans later in this chapter). I could fill pages making up plans for all kinds of situations, but I know that is not necessary. Once you see how simple this is, I have every confidence you will be able to create a wardrobe plan that works for each person in your family.

Career Woman Wardrobe Plan

3-piece suit—skirt, jacket, and pants (navy or black)

3 skirts (taupe, gray, black)

2 dresses (one should be a basic black dress)

5 blouses (at least one button-front shirt)

2 blazer-type jackets

3 pairs slacks

3 coats (rain, between seasons, and winter for your area)

2 sweatshirts

5 T-shirts

2 jeans

2 jackets (one sporty, one parka-type)

2 pairs pumps

2 pairs low shoes

1 pair sneakers

Career Man Wardrobe Plan

2-piece suit (navy or black)

5 shirts

5 ties

2 sports jackets

3 pairs slacks

2 coats (trench for rain and winter coat)

2 sweatshirts

5 T-shirts

2 jeans

2 jackets (one sporty, one parka-type)

2 pairs shoes (dress, casual)

1 pair sneakers

Closet Sweep

While many items in your wardrobe are not right for you and should be purged, you may be surprised to discover how many items you have already to plug into your wardrobe plan. However, before you can do this effectively, you may need to separate the useful from the get-rid-ofs. Not easy. Believe me.

I find it difficult to get rid of anything with a perceived value. I think that as long as I store it there's a chance that one day I may actually wear it. And I tend to hang on to things that hold promise because they look so great on the hanger. We both know that it's time to give them up. I have a painless way to do this.

Move everything out of your closet and your drawers too, if you can manage. Put everything in a spare room closet or armoire if at all possible. Do a clean sweep of your closet, leaving it empty. If you cannot manage that, push everything to one side to make a visual separation. For clothes and out-fits to earn a spot in your clean closet and empty drawers:

1. Each item must be listed on your wardrobe plan.
2. You must actually wear it.

In a short time, you should be able to figure out what you wear regularly and what you don't. You can safely purge the losers, unless it's a seasonal issue (your winter coat is fabulous; you just don't wear it in the summer). Take the clothes that are not right for you to a donation location or consignment shop, price them for a garage sale or to sell them on eBay, or arrange a clothing swap with your friends and relatives.

Whatever method you choose, be strong. You can do this, and oh, what a sense of accomplishment you will have once you have completed a successful purge.

Putting the Plan into Action

You have a uniform based on your colors, clothing personal-ity, and body type (it can be a loose idea for now), and you have a wardrobe plan. You know with certainty what, if anything, you need to flesh out your plan. Now you are in the position to buy what you need and want what you have. You have options—more options now than ever before.

Because you need a pair of khaki slacks in a particular style, you can shop sales, consignment shops, thrift stores, eBay, Target, or Nordstrom's semiannual sale. If you are re-placing a pair of pants that fit well and you've enjoyed for a long time, make a note of the brand and style number. Now you can shop strategically. When you find them at the right price, you will have no question whether it is a good purchase.

Your confidence will soar as your clothing costs plummet. Why? Because you will avoid buying five pairs of the wrong pants on your way to finally getting the right pair.

Get the Right Measurements

Before you buy another piece of clothing, you need eight critical measurements and a cloth tape measure to carry with you at all times. With this information, you can take all the hassle out of fitting rooms by taking a few strategic measurements of those pants or that top while they are hanging on the rack.

Why try it on if there is no chance it will fit? Or look at it this way. Each item you take with you into the fitting room will have a high likelihood of being right for you because before you even try it on you will have determined that you need it and can afford it and that it is the right color, shape, and size for you.

Here are the eight standard measurements you need for yourself, your spouse, your children, and anyone else for whom you purchase clothes:

1. Shoulder to shoulder: from the edge of one shoulder to the edge of the other shoulder
2. Bust: under your arms, around the fullest part of your chest
3. Natural waist: at your navel
4. Low waist: approximately one inch below your natural waist
5. High hip: four to five inches below your natural waist
6. Low hip: eight to nine inches below your natural waist

7. Thigh: at its widest point

8. Rise: from your natural waist down to your crotch, holding the tape a little loose, through your legs up to the waistband in the back; repeat for low waist

Okay, you've got your measurements and your cloth tape in your bag or pocket. You need a pair of jeans. You check the rack and see a pair of jeans in your size (a dubious distinction, as every manufacturer sizes items differently, especially jeans). You know from your measurements that your hips are forty-four inches. You whip out your tape measure and measure side to side across the widest place. You multiply by two and come up with forty-one inches. You can put that pair back on the rack and move on. You don't need to waste your time in the fitting room. Those pants will not fit.

You can continue measuring pants on the rack, saving yourself time and frustration, until you come to a pair that measures correctly for you. You check the rise, and it's at least in the right ballpark. Now you have a pair of jeans with a high likelihood of fitting. You try on that pair.

Find a Tailor

Now that you understand how important it is that your clothes fit well, you also will understand that ready-to-wear clothes for adults aren't always ready to wear. Having a good tailor who can lift a hem, take in a seam, and shorten a sleeve is vital. With this option, so many more opportunities will open to you. A good tailor can take a garment down two sizes, which will come as good news if you find a jacket or skirt that is perfect in every way for your wardrobe plan but is two sizes too big.

The cost for altering clothing can vary significantly from city to suburbs, so it's best to check with several tailors to get a lay of the land. Compare the costs at two or three alterations shops for replacing a zipper, changing the hem in a dress, and shortening a pair of slacks with cuffs.

If you do not know of a good tailor in your area, check with your local dry cleaners. Many now have on-site tailoring services. A good tailor has a changing room available because he or she must check for fit and mark for alterations while you are wearing the garment. No changing room? Keep looking.

If you have a sewing machine and are inclined to learn a skill, sign up for a class in basic tailoring. You'll bless the day you made the decision to learn how to make your own alterations.

Know Where to Buy

The best thing about having a uniform and knowing your measurements is that a whole new world of opportunity for acquiring clothes is now open to you.

Let's say your wardrobe plan calls for a brown wool herringbone jacket with a black velvet collar. You have a specific need. It doesn't matter where you get this jacket as long as it is the right style, color, and size (or can easily be made the right size to fit you exactly).

Consignment, outlet, retail (yes, they do have sales!), thrift, discount, vintage, warehouse club, high-end, even eBay—all of these places are possibilities for you.

CONSIGNMENT SHOPS

You'll find the cream of the crop in clothing if you look for these stores in tony areas. Also known as resale, reclothery, and repeats, this secondary market, which offers gently worn clothes for women primarily, but also for men and children, is gaining acceptance and popularity.

Consignment stores run the gamut from no frills to opulent. What they share are great prices on high-quality, excellent clothes. Items in consignment shops are typically priced at least 60 percent off the original retail price. You can expect a higher level of quality and care with clothes on consignment than in thrift stores. Sellers are required to deliver the items freshly cleaned and still in dry-cleaner bags. Some stores accept only clothes from a standard list of designers, while others may have a broader list but require garments to be in pristine condition.

A really great consignment shop has a fast turnover of product. Your best clue for how quickly a shop turns over its inventory is its window displays. If they change every week, you know it's an active store.

Outlets

It used to be that an outlet store was at the back of a factory where slightly irregular items, samples, and overstocks of first-run products were sold for a fraction of the new retail price. Talk about bargains!

But that has all changed. Nowadays, some major retailers have more outlet stores than regular retail stores, and that is a clue about where the inventory originates. Some retailers manufacture low-end discount lines just for their outlets. So outlets definitely can be a mixed bag.

An example of an authentic outlet store is DanskoOutlet. com, where you can buy seconds direct from the manufacturer for 30 percent to 50 percent off regular retail prices. These are not first-quality shoes—they have visible flaws.

However, the company happily shows up-close examples of these flaws. I've purchased more than a few pairs of shoes here, and the flaws are minuscule, if even noticeable.

Then there are the outlets that are little more than a repository for last season's leftovers and for flawed items that are too good for the landfill but not good enough for the real store. Perhaps the items were mislabeled at the factory or mis-sized. Perhaps they were cut off-grain. That might not matter while the garment is hanging on the rack, but it will never hang just right, feel just right, or look just right even if it measures correctly. All that to say, you have to be cautious. Never buy something from an outlet store that you have not tried on. If you are diligent, you can find some real treasures in outlet stores. Even then, if something does not have a place in your wardrobe plan, step away from it.

RETAIL STORES

If you wait for the big sales at mainstream retailers, you can stretch your clothing dollars to cover first-quality, in-season clothing. Inquire with the sales force as to when a particular line or item might be marked down. In fact, don't be surprised if they offer to put the item aside pending the sale or call you when the sale is announced. Most retailers have extensive websites where you can peruse the season's offerings and devise a strategy. You can do a great deal of research without leaving home.

THRIFT STORES

These days, thrift stores, also known as secondhand or used-clothing stores, vary as much as retail stores. Some are so fancy you'd think you were in a unique boutique of some type. Others are . . . well, down and dirty. What they share in common is that their entire inventory has been donated for a charitable cause, as opposed to consignment stores, whose offerings are generally more gently worn and a portion of the sale returns to the original owner.

One thrift store shopper sadly told me that thrift store bargains are not what they used to be, as these stores now have more inventory from which to choose. They can be more discriminating in what they are willing to accept in donations. The prices reflect this.

While thrift stores are still a viable venue for acquiring clothes that fit into your wardrobe plan, you need to be wise in your assessments. And, of course, once you have an alterations service or tailor at the ready, exact fit is not as critical as quality. Just make sure you have your eight measurements and a measuring tape handy.

DEEP DISCOUNTERS

Stores like T.J.Maxx, Marshalls, Stein Mart, and Ross move merchandise like it's going out of style! There are some good deals to be found provided you happen to be there at the right time and are willing to dig. The real steals are often found in the back on these stores' clearance racks.

Brace yourself, though. You will find rips and missing buttons and all kinds of challenges. But if you approach this with your tailor in mind, your measurements in tow, and your tape measure ready, you just might find a gem. These stores carry designer labels and high-end merchandise that for one reason or another couldn't make it on Fifth Avenue.

A good rule of thumb is that a professional tailor can take a garment down two sizes without losing the classic lines and proportion. More than that is a real challenge and expensive. But if that $350 Ralph Lauren wool blazer in the exact color and style you have been searching for has two buttons missing and a ripped lining and is a size 12 when you wear a 10, don't be so quick to walk on by. At $19.99, it may be the buried treasure you hoped to find.

DISCOUNT DEPARTMENT STORES

Kmart, Target, Walmart, and Kohl's (to name just a few) offer a haven of bargains, particularly for children's clothes. Remember to always match quality with need.

A growing child does not need quality clothing designed to wear well for many years. For kids, shop for low-end clothes that will hold up as long as needed. These stores' sales can make the bargains even sweeter. Find out a store's schedule for marking things down. One reader wrote to say her Target marks items down every Tuesday evening. She times her trips accordingly.

ONLINE AUCTIONS

While there are many online auction sites, eBay.com is the most well known, and clothing is one of its largest categories. You really can find just about every type, brand, designer, color, and style of garment imaginable on eBay. But you have to be careful.

You don't know where that garment is coming from. It might be brand-new hanging in someone else's closet. It might be brand-new, first-quality offered by a small distributor of that particular brand of clothes. Or it might be part of a truckload of store returns from Bloomingdales. It might be stained, hopelessly stretched out of shape, faded, or reeking of cigarette smoke. You just don't know. But you can find out. Provided you are willing to follow very cautious guidelines (as explained in chap. 3), you may discover you can build your entire wardrobe from eBay. The secret is to know your prices and your products.

Take the two brands of clothes that I buy on eBay. I know these designers and manufacturers inside and out. I go to a local department store to touch and try on. I know the specific colors by name, how the sizes run, and the difference between, for example, what one designer calls a "tunic" and a "top." When a piece from this line shows up on eBay, I know exactly what it is and how it fits. A quick communication with the seller gives me a good idea of the origin of the garment and what I can expect to receive.

A friend of mine enjoys the Tommy Bahama line of men's clothes. When I recommended he bid for the items he needs on eBay, he was more than a little skeptical. But he did as I suggested and visited a department store to get familiar with the different styles of pants and so forth. Sure enough, when items he wanted hit the eBay auction, he was able to buy them for far less than half of the new price, including the shipping.

Clothes for Kids

Using the basic principles of color, shape, and style, create wardrobe plans for every member of your family, even your kids—especially for growing kids. It simply does not make economic sense to pay full retail for clothes that will be worn for such a short time.

Recent studies warn parents that kids who've been given too much too soon grow up to be adults who have difficulty coping with life's disappointments. They have a distorted sense of entitlement that gets in the way of success both in the workplace and in relationships.

Psychologists say parents who overindulge their kids may be setting them up to be more vulnerable to future anxiety and depression. Overindulging children with clothes, toys, and possessions can affect them as adults with higher incidents of depression and divorce. Just because you can afford to fill your child's closet with designer duds doesn't mean you should. Sometimes it's harder to say no than yes.

To keep yourself on track and from going overboard on impulse buys (oh, it's so cute), make a simple wardrobe plan for each child. Then stick to it. Here are examples.

Boy's Wardrobe Plan

4 washable pants (two jeans, two pants)

3–5 shirts

4–5 T-shirts

2 sweatshirts

1 light jacket

1 heavy coat

1 pair sneakers

1 pair shoes

Girl's Wardrobe Plan

4 washable pants (two jeans, two pants)

3–5 tops

3 T-shirts

2 skirts

1–2 dresses

2 sweatshirts

1 light jacket

1 heavy coat

1 pair sneakers

2 pairs shoes

Children don't need many clothes. The more they have, the more your laundry will pile up and the more items will find their way to the back of the closet, never to be seen again. Too many choices translate into clutter, guilt, and waste.

Basic colors. A child's wardrobe functions on the same principles of color as an adult's. But instead of seeing all colors in that child's natural palette as candidates for his or her clothes, stick to a few basic colors. You'll be able to mix and match with ease, make more outfits, and coordinate with other clothes already in your child's closet.

Hand-me-downs. My best advice is to accept gratefully any trades, swaps, or outright gifts of clothes from relatives, friends, or others. And when you're done with those clothes, pass them along to others as appropriate.

Strategic gifting. If grandparents and others give your children gifts for Christmas and birthdays, suggest the items that will plug in the gaps in each child's wardrobe plan. Most people appreciate specifics of size, color, and style.

Consignment and resale. Stores just for kids, from newborn through preteen, are opening up in communities everywhere. And why not? Kids grow so fast that often their clothes are barely worn. Consignment is a great way to turn gently worn items into cash.

One such example is the national chain of consignment stores called Once Upon a Child (see OUAC.com for store locator). You'll be amazed how many new-with-tags designer labels you'll find at these stores—baby furniture and equipment too—all at prices close to half off retail. An online consignment store for children is ThredUp.com.

Now and later. When you come across a particularly excellent sale for something that works perfectly for your child, consider buying that item in several sizes for now and for next year too.

Online deals. eBay is especially rich with high-quality, designer-brand, excellent-condition clothes for kids. Once you peruse the bargains available, you may find it impossible to pay full retail elsewhere.

Other online sites also offer excellent bargains direct to the public from time to time. An excellent example is the well-known OshKosh brand at OshKoshBGosh.com. Look for the markdowns; just make sure you consider the shipping costs too.

8

Attack of the Killer Fees

Money is not just pieces of paper or electronic blips
with prices attached. It is far more: Our fondest
hopes, our most fervent dreams, our worst night-
mares, all balled up into an explosively emotional
package.

Jason Zweig, columnist

L isten. Hear that loud whooshing sound? It's money
being sucked out of millions of individual bank accounts, credit card accounts, and mortgage repayment plans
in fees—big, bad, budget-busting fees—most of them completely hidden from the consumers who are paying them.

So take a guess. How much of your household income
disappears out of your bank account each year just in service

fees so that you can have access to your money? A conservative estimate is that a typical family in the US pays between $600 and $1,000 a year in service fees alone.[1] This figure doesn't include interest or punitive fees (late, overlimit, and so on)—only the fees you pay to have access to your money.

You can stop the attack of the killer fees on your money. You don't have to contribute to banks' and credit card companies' huge profits (more than 30 percent of the $100 billion in profits the banks made in 2003 came from fees) to have checking and savings accounts, a credit card, and ATM access.

By following a few simple strategies, you can easily keep that $600 to $1,000 from being sucked out of your accounts every year. It is possible to enjoy all the safety and convenience of banking, credit card, and ATM services without paying a cent in fees. But before I can show you how to do that, we need to sort through the myriad of fees being imposed on you—most of them buried in the fine print.

Fees on financial services fall into two categories: service fees and punitive fees. Service fees are the fees banks, credit unions, and credit grantors charge for their services. Punitive fees are "punishment" fees charged to customers who break the rules.

Bank Accounts

You signed up for a free checking account. So what are all those fees piled up at the bottom of your account statement every month? Maybe it's time to take a closer look.

Service fees. These fees (sometimes called maintenance fees) on bank checking accounts can include a flat monthly fee, a per-check fee, a fee for speaking to an account representative ($3 per conversation at one of the nation's largest banks), a fee for checking your account balance by phone, a fee for using an out-of-network ATM, a fee for receiving copies of your paid checks, and a fee for using telephone banking.

Have you analyzed your bank statement recently? That's where you will find these kinds of mystery fees. Question everything! You should not have to pay a cent to have access to your own money.

Minimum balance fees. Many checking accounts have minimum balance requirements. In exchange for your promise to keep plenty of money in your account at all times, you receive interest on the balance. If you allow the balance to fall below the predetermined amount, a penalty fee is assessed or the interest is withheld or both.

Overdraft fees. Fees for bouncing a check can be horrendous. And with more banks availing themselves of the provisions of the law, your paper check can now clear as fast as a debit card transaction. Depending on what type of arrangement you have with your bank, a single bounced check could cost you a small fortune. First, there's the overdraft fee. You'll get this no matter what. And if the check is paid from your overdraft protection account or with the bank's funds, the fees plus interest will begin to pile up quickly.

ATM fees. Some financial institutions do not charge a fee to use an ATM provided you use that bank's machine. However, this is not universal. Some banks charge a fee to use even their bank's machine and an additional fee if you use an outside ATM.

Free Bank Accounts

Nearly every bank and credit union used to offer some kind of personal "free" checking account. They had to, because that's what the competition was doing. But those days are rapidly coming to an end. It is quite difficult to find a truly free bank account these days, although it is still possible.

Credit union. This is a good option for finding a free checking account. Unlike a bank, which is a for-profit corporation, a credit union is a not-for-profit corporation whose purpose is to make money for its members and account holders. The profits of a credit union are used to reduce the cost of services, including interest rates on loans, and are also returned to the members in the form of dividends. To find a credit union you can join, go to CreditUnion.coop and click on "Locate a Credit Union."

Be sure to ask all the right questions. Is there a minimum balance requirement? Is there a charge for personalized checks? (If so, order directly from a check printer like ChecksInTheMail.com). What are the overdraft penalty fees? What are the fees to use ATMs, and what are the restrictions?

Local independent bank. Your best option for a truly free checking account in a local bank is with one that is independent. Unless you travel a lot and need access to a branch of your bank in every major city, there is no benefit to banking with a big national bank.

USAA Federal Savings Bank. This is it—the only place I know where you can get a 100 percent free checking account that includes free checks, free postage-paid envelopes, no charge whatsoever to access your money, and interest too.

This bank is a cross between a bank and a credit union because it is owned by its 4.3 million members—many of them connected to the US military in some way. However, the banking services are available to the public.

USAA Bank offers a free checking account with no conditions, minimums, or requirements; free personalized checks; free deposit slips; and free postage-paid and preaddressed envelopes to make deposits.

Located in San Antonio, Texas, USAA Federal Savings Bank does not have branch offices. But USAA can be your branch bank no matter where you live. Online banking is available 24/7. You mail deposits in postage-paid envelopes or make automatic deposits if you prefer (it's not required). You can use an ATM anywhere, and USAA will reimburse you $1.50 per ATM use up to ten times per month. This amount will show up on your statement as a credit. If you use an ATM more than ten times a month, you need to evaluate your ATM usage and adjust accordingly.

USAA pays interest on checking accounts, a rate higher than some banks pay for basic savings accounts, but only on balances of more than $1,000. That's not a minimum balance of any kind or an average balance. Your account is scanned every day, and if the balance is $1,000 or more, they pay you interest for that day.

You can add online bill-paying privileges to your free checking account. There is a small monthly fee of $4.95 for this service. But if you have automatic deposit of your paycheck, even online bill paying is completely free.

USAA offers overdraft protection that is tied to either your savings account or a credit card account. If you use your overdraft protection by drawing on your credit or savings account, there is no fee. The service to transfer the funds is free. If you do not have overdraft protection, checks are returned

"NSF" and a $29 fee is assessed. That's the most reasonable penalty structure you will find at any bank or credit union.

Joining USAA is tricky, so stay with me. When you access the website (USAA.com), you will be confused. I guarantee it. Everything you read on the site will lead you to believe that unless you are presently an active member of the US military—or have a connection through a family member— you are not eligible to join USAA. But this is not true. You are eligible. Let me explain.

USAA has a huge family of financial services; banking is just one of those services. However (and trust me on this), the banking services are available to anyone over age eighteen with a Social Security number. All you need is a membership number. You must make a one-time toll-free phone call to 800-531-2265 to get a membership number so that you can open a new checking or savings account. Automated service is always available, and customer service representatives are available Monday through Friday, 7:30 a.m.–10:00 p.m. CT; Saturday, 8:00 a.m.–6:00 p.m. CT; Sunday, 1:00 p.m.–6:00 p.m. CT. Once you have your membership number, you can either ask for an application to be mailed to you or you can go to USAA.com and click on "Register Now."

Once you have established a password and log-in account, you can open a checking account online. You will have the option to receive an ATM card or a debit card to go with your account. Once a member, you are also eligible to open a savings account that will earn a better rate of interest than the checking account. You can make transfers between your USAA bank accounts online or by phone. You will receive your debit card or ATM card and deposit envelopes in the mail, as well as a supply of personalized checks.

Credit Card Accounts

Service fees. Many credit card issuers charge an annual fee ranging from $35 to $300 or more. More companies than ever before are also tacking on a monthly maintenance fee of $6 to $9. These are not punishment fees, but they sure look like it. They are fees charged simply for the privilege of spending with plastic.

Interest rates. The penalty fee with the greatest impact on a credit card account is, of course, the interest on the unpaid balance—the penalty for living beyond your means. It can be steep, and the interest rate on credit card accounts is always variable.

The fine print on the initial credit card application or the sheet that came with the credit card itself reveals the interest rate structure, complicated as it may be. First, there is the interest on balance transfers, then the interest on new purchases. The interest on cash advances is always different and usually the highest rate allowed in that state. Many cards also have a "default rate" built in, which is the interest rate that will kick in if the cardholder defaults on any of the provisions of the credit card agreement. A default can occur with something as minor as being five minutes late with a payment.

Late payment fees. Making a credit card payment late can be deadly. It's like knocking down the first domino. It starts with a severe late fee of $35 or more added to your account.

Overlimit fees. Most credit card accounts have a credit limit. And unlike years ago when you could not charge beyond your limit, banks and credit card companies are quite happy for a customer to break through that barrier. They happily charge you interest on the growing balance and then sock

147

you with an overlimit penalty fee of $29 to $35 every month until the balance is reduced sufficiently to be under your limit.

Don't Let This Happen to You

A late fee added to a credit card account can push an almost-maxed-out account balance overlimit, which triggers an automatic overlimit penalty fee. Together they can add $70 to an account balance.

The following month the minimum monthly payment is not sufficient to bring the balance below the credit limit, so another overlimit penalty of $35 is charged. Even if you don't use the card at all, the balance grows all on its own and at a rate faster than the minimum payments can bring it down. But wait! It gets worse.

Remember, a late fee started all of this, and being late even one time gives the company a window of opportunity to increase the interest rate on the account to its default rate, which for many card issuers is now the highest rate allowed in the account holder's state—28 percent or more. This snowball effect can be an unrelenting punishment for the cardholder. The problem is that the card company encourages and enables this by allowing a customer to charge past his or her credit limit. And if that's not enough, late payments wreak havoc on one's credit score.

Free Credit Card

You need one good, all-purpose credit card. Just one. That card should have no annual fee and a grace period of at least twenty-five days and should be accepted in many places (VISA and MasterCard are accepted most widely). If you use it, faithfully pay the balance in full long before the due date. Now you have a totally fee-free credit card.

Where can you find a card like that (if you do not have one already)? Log on to IndexCreditCards.com, a site that lists all current credit card offerings. You will find a fairly lengthy list of cards for your consideration.

As a member of USAA Federal Savings Bank (honest, I'm not their spokesperson), you can apply for their USAA MasterCard. It fits all of the fee-free specifications plus has a relatively low interest rate and penalty fee structure. Once you are a member of USAA's banking services (see above for how to join), you can apply for the card at USAA.com.

Stop the Penalty Fees

By now you know how not to pay service fees for financial services. And now you want to know how to stop paying penalty fees. This is easy. Stop breaking the rules!

Stop bouncing checks; stop making late payments; stop pushing the limits on your credit cards. Stop allowing balances to revolve on your credit cards so that you are paying interest.

If you are carrying a lot of debt, you may not be able to change the interest part of your equation overnight. But you can renew your resolve to get out of debt. Every month, you will see that balance come down until you are free—free of consumer debt, free of penalty fees, and free of fees that erode and nibble away at your money.

9

Home, Sweet,
Paid-for Home

A home of our own is still the rock on which our
hopes are built. Homeownership is a state of mind.
It's your piece of the earth. It's where a family's
toes grow roots. It's where the flowers are yours.

Jane Bryant Quinn,
Making the Most of Your Money

B uying a home is likely the single best way to build wealth
on your ordinary income. But homeownership is about
more than financial appreciation. Putting down roots and
raising a family on land you know is yours offer emotional
fulfillment and security too.

As wonderful as it is to buy your own home, you do not want to spend the rest of your life as a home buyer. You want to be a homeowner in every sense of the word. Paying your mortgage in full is your number one goal as a homeowner and what I focus on in this chapter. As you are about to learn, you can own your home sooner than you ever dreamed possible and save a lot of dough in the process.

The reason you want to work your way out of a mortgage is so that you can enjoy living "free" in retirement. Rent goes on forever; your mortgage payments eventually come to a stop. Your goal should be to own a home in full before you stop earning an active income.

The interest you pay on your mortgage and your property taxes are tax deductible. This means that, for once, the government is putting money in your pocket by subsidizing the purchase of your house. Current mortgage rates are still low by historical standards, and buying a house at a fixed rate means you know what your housing costs will be in the future until your mortgage is paid off.

Buying a house is a kind of forced savings plan. Each month, a percentage of the mortgage payment goes to the principal. It's a trivial amount in the first years, but it increases throughout the term of the mortgage. This is money on top of the increased value of the house each year, which is what makes this winning combination the best investment available to you.

Sweet Equity

Every mortgage has three important elements: market value, principal balance, and equity. Market value is the amount your house would sell for today. Principal balance is the amount you owe. Equity is the amount of money you would have in your pocket if you sold the house today, after paying off the principal balance.

Historically, a house in the US appreciates 4 percent to 5 percent per year. Of course, the figure varies from neighborhood to neighborhood and region to region, but it's a good rule of thumb. Do the math. If you buy a $200,000 house with 20 percent down ($40,000) and it appreciates at 5 percent per year, the value increases $10,000 in the first year. That's $10,000 on a $40,000 down payment or a return of 25 percent.

Each month during the payback process, the principal balance goes down and the equity goes up. But this is the wonderful thing. The equity is fueled by two factors: appreciation (the home's value goes up just because houses generally become more valuable over time) and the shrinking mortgage. Each month you own a tiny bit more of the home. That is the definition of equity. Your equity continues to grow until that wonderful day when your mortgage is at $0 and your equity is at 100 percent.

You don't have to own the same home for your entire mortgage payback time. You can move your equity from one home to the next. When you sell, you use the equity from that house as the down payment on the next home. With each move, you take more equity, making a larger down payment and requiring a smaller mortgage. The mistake would be to make only the minimum down payment on the next house and spend your equity on something else. Then you would need a much larger mortgage and would put your final mortgage payoff date much farther into the future.

Provided you are careful to keep moving all of the equity from your prior home to the next home, your equity will continue to grow rapidly, and you will eventually own a home free and clear.

Rapid Mortgage Repayment

Perhaps you have heard of or have a "biweekly" mortgage payment plan. Your mortgage lender or a third party may have approached you to switch to this kind of plan. The basic principle is that by paying half of your mortgage payment every two weeks instead of all of it once a month, you can drastically reduce the amount of interest and repay the mortgage in far fewer years.

It's true. Here's an example. Let's say your monthly mortgage payment is $1,000. In one year, you make twelve payments—$12,000 each year. If you pay one-half of a payment ($500) every two weeks, or biweekly, you will make twenty-six half payments in a year, or a total of $13,000, the equivalent of thirteen monthly payments. Therein lies the secret of the biweekly mortgage payment plan—making that additional monthly payment over a year's time.

A biweekly payment schedule typically reduces a mortgage payback time by five or six years, saving the borrower many thousands of dollars in interest. No doubt a biweekly payment schedule is a painless and effective way to save a boatload of interest.

The theory is excellent, but there is a problem. Biweekly payment plans offered by mortgage lenders are fraught with fees. Typically, there's a conversion fee to change from a monthly plan to a biweekly plan. Often the conversion fee is about $400. Then there's a $4 or $5 fee tacked onto each biweekly payment. If that doesn't sound like much, figure it out. It adds up. In fact, the initial fee plus the payment fees, if applied to your mortgage instead of boosting the lender's profit margins, could knock another year or so off your payback time.

There is also an inherent yet often overlooked problem with converting to a biweekly plan: You're stuck. Once you convert, you must continue the biweekly schedule or be zinged with late fees. And if you want to go back to a monthly plan, there will be fees for that too.

The good news is that you can do the same thing with your mortgage payback time and save all that interest too—without fees and without asking your lender for permission. You can also start now, and if in the future you are met with a season of financial challenges, you can pull back to your original payment schedule. You'll suffer no penalty or conversion fees. And you won't have to ask permission of your lender. Here's how.

Each month when you make your regularly scheduled mortgage payment, write a second check for one-twelfth of one regular mortgage payment. Using the simple scenario above, write a check for $1,000 for your regular mortgage payment. At the same time, write a second check for $83.33 ($\frac{1}{12}$ of $1,000). On this second check, write on the memo line "principal prepayment only." Send in both checks. You have complied with your lender's requirement of making at least one full payment each month and have taken advantage of the fact that your mortgage does not have a prepayment penalty provision.

Do this each month, and by the end of a year, you will have made the equivalent of thirteen monthly payments, twelve payments as scheduled with one full payment extra going to prepay the principal. Bingo! You have just accomplished the same action as a biweekly payment schedule on your terms—without fees. The nice thing about taking control of your own accelerated payment schedule in this way is that you can stop and start up again at will. It's up to you, not the lender.

Pay Down or Pay Ahead

Whenever you send more than the amount of your regular payment, you should write in the memo area of the check and also attach a note explaining what it is for; otherwise, how will your lender know what to do with it?

Borrowers send extra money to their mortgage companies for two common reasons: (1) to pay down the principal balance or (2) to make payments ahead.

When you send an additional payment or amount to pay down the principal balance, your loan balance goes down. But you still have to make the next scheduled payment. Let's say you make your regular mortgage payment in April plus three extra payments. You enclose a note that the additional payments are to pay down the principal balance. You will still have a payment due in May, June, and July, as scheduled.

On the other hand, let's assume for a moment that you sent those three extra payments for a different reason. You are going to Europe for the summer and don't want to have to worry about making mortgage payments. It's just easier to make them now so you can forget about them. In this scenario, you want to pay the account ahead. Attaching a note to the additional payments will tell the lender to apply them to the May, June, and July payments. You'll be back before the August payment is due.

Home, Sweet, Paid-for Home

If you are not clear about how you want those three extra payments handled, the lender might assume you want to pay down the principal balance. You head off on your trip assuming you've made your mortgage payments. Of course, you don't get the late notices because you're not home. You arrive home only to learn that your home is in foreclosure for failure to pay.

You cannot assume the mortgage company will automatically pay your account ahead if you do not send clear instructions. Nor can you assume they will know to pay down the principal balance. Some lenders will simply return additional payments if it is not clear how they are to be handled. Others automatically apply additional sums to future payments, defaulting to the lender's benefit, which would be to pay ahead.

Do not staple your instructions to your check. Use a paper clip instead. And make sure you also abbreviate your instructions on the check itself. But don't leave it there. Follow up in a couple of weeks to make sure the transaction was handled per your instructions. If you get a monthly statement, just wait for it. If all you have are a stack of coupons, and your lender sends a statement once a year, make sure you call to verify that your account is being handled properly.

Two Notes of Caution

You should not even think about prepaying your mortgage until you have amassed a respectable emergency fund equal to six months' living expenses and have paid off all of your unsecured debts. Prepaying your mortgage before achieving those goals is foolish, because when something unexpected happens, you'll run to credit cards—or, worse, your home's

157

equity—for a bail out if you do not have an emergency fund to fall back on.

Another common mistake first-time home buyers make is getting in over their heads. They commit to more house than they can afford. But they don't realize this fact because they allow a real-estate broker or mortgage lender to tell them how much they can afford through a process called prequalification. How do these people know? They look strictly at your current income and compare that to current market and economic conditions. However, your current conditions could change, and if you have a payment that stretches you to the limit, you could be in big trouble down the road.

I want you to consider a better way. Find out what you can afford to pay each month in principal and interest through the prequalifying process. Let's say you can qualify for $2,000 payments, which will get you a $375,000 house with a 20 percent down payment at 4.5 percent interest for thirty years. But you don't want to pay for a house for thirty years.

So you tell the broker to show you homes in the $213,600 range (the median price for an existing single-family home in the US as of May 2014,[1] which in some areas wouldn't even buy a garage, but this is only an example, okay?) with $983 payments. It might be a smaller fixer-upper in a less desirable neighborhood, but that's just fine because you have a plan.

You are not going to make the required $983 payment each month. You are going to make $2,000 payments—the payments the lender said you could afford. Instead of taking thirty years, you will pay the mortgage in full in just eight years and avoid paying a ton of interest.

You're still young. You have plenty of time to sell this house and apply the entire sale price toward the down payment on a nicer house that is (you guessed it) half the house you qualify for. You'll own the next house in about five years because you will have a larger down payment than required. Of course, this is an estimate because I am not clairvoyant, but the principle holds true.

This is such a smart way to become a homeowner because you opt for less house in the beginning of your home-ownership career. And for your willingness to start small, you are rewarded handsomely because you pay far less interest in the long run and become mortgage-free much sooner.

Refinancing

About the only thing trickier than figuring out if you should refinance your home's mortgage to take advantage of lower interest rates is addressing this dilemma in a couple of snappy, exciting, and terribly interesting paragraphs. But first, let's review some basic fundamental truths about a home mortgage.

Mortgages are meant to be paid off. The reason home mortgages in the US are based on a thirty-year payback is so you will own your home free and clear before you retire. One problem with refinancing is that without weighing the long-term effects, borrowers reset the clock back to a thirty-year payback period.

There was a time when "burning the mortgage" was common practice. It was a noble, albeit common, accomplishment. Have you ever been invited to a mortgage burning party? My point exactly. Making the last payment on a mortgage is a bit of a rarity.

To Refinance or Not to Refinance

To determine if you should refinance your mortgage, you need to look at the big picture, not only the monthly payment. A drop of two points in your interest rate could reduce your monthly payment by hundreds of dollars. If you look only at the payment, there's no question that refinancing is a good move. But you can't stop there. You need to look at the total payback on the proposed refinance and compare that to the total amount required to finish paying your mortgage at the current rate.

Let's say you have a thirty-year mortgage on $100,000 at 8 percent interest. Your monthly principal and interest payment is $734. After ten years of faithfully paying your mortgage payment each month, you have an outstanding balance of $87,872.

You get an opportunity to refinance that balance at 6 percent with new payments of $527. You're just about ready to go for the deal because you like the idea of having more than $200 each month for something else when I come bursting into your life with a great big cautionary flag. Before you make your decision, you need to look at the big picture. If you stay with your current mortgage, you will make 240 more payments of $734 for a total of $176,160. If you refinance, you will make 360 payments (refinancing typically restarts the clock) of $527 or a total payback of $189,720. Add to this the costs of refinancing (they vary greatly but could be several thousands of dollars for an appraisal, loan fees, recording fees, title insurance, and so on, and if added to the principal amount they will also accrue interest), some of which may be required up front. There is some value to paying less each month, but rarely does that trump adding ten more years to your payback time.

Chances are high that the lender offering the refinance will convince you to finance more than just the outstanding balance on your current mortgage. "Cashing out" some or all of your equity is in the lender's best interest but rarely yours.

Suggestions that you should take out money to complete any number of home improvements will be compelling. Many people take this opportunity to get their hands on cash to pay off credit card debt, to pay for college tuition, or to pay for some other life event. Before long, the $87,872 you owed on your home becomes $100,000 or $200,000 or more.

You will make a serious error if you use your equity as cash to spend on what you want now. If you do, you will watch your precious equity go up in smoke and will take a giant step away from your dream of paying your mortgage in full so you are a real homeowner.

The promise of a low interest rate on the refinance makes this look quite inviting. I don't need to give you more numbers to prove just how costly a refinance can be under these circumstances, including using your equity. Not only will you actually increase your monthly payments, but you'll also extend the time it takes to pay off your mortgage. In the meantime, should you fall on hard times, you may have trouble making the much larger payment. That opens the door to foreclosure and losing your home altogether.

Let me suggest a way that refinancing under the terms above could be beneficial. First, insist that you want to refinance only your outstanding balance, or in our example $87,872. The temptation will be great to get your hands on some of your equity, but curb that urge. Your new payments will be $527 as described above. Each month when you make this new payment, write an additional check for

$207, directing this amount to be applied to "principal pre-payment only."

You are paying the same amount you've been paying each month for the past ten years ($527 + $207 = $734). Nothing changes there. However, and this is the good part, you will have a total payback of only $134,327 (that's a savings of more than $55,000 in interest), and even better, you will pay off your mortgage completely in about fifteen years, not the twenty years you are looking at now. This is how refinancing can benefit you in a big way—not pump up the lender's bottom line and income stream.

Remember, always consider the total payback not just the new monthly payment when you evaluate a refinance. It is easy to figure this out if you have the right calculators. In the calculations above, I used the "Loan Calculator with Amortization Schedule" and "Debt Investment Calculator" at DebtProofLiving.com. It was simple. These are two of the dozens of useful calculators my website members enjoy.

Variable versus Fixed Interest

The illustration above assumed mortgages with fixed interest rates. If you have a variable-interest or interest-only mortgage, your motivation to refinance becomes more complicated. You need to refinance into a fixed-rate mortgage as soon as feasible.

If you got into the current mortgage because you could not handle the payment on a fixed-rate loan at the time, you should be in better shape now to do that. Because variable-rate mortgages are tied to indexes that reflect current economic conditions, even if you have caps that keep the rate from increasing more than say 2 percent in a year, you are in a risky position. I suggest that you look toward refinancing your current outstanding balance at the best fixed rate you can find.

Owning a home is a smart move for all kinds of reasons. Mortgage payments force you to save. You know you are building something for the future. You get deductions for taxes and interest, and you can paint the rooms any color you like. But above all, homeownership allows you to look forward to the day you'll live mortgage-free. Play your cards right and that day will arrive sooner than later.

10

Remember When
Talk Was Cheap?

Discipline comes through self-control. . . . Before
you can control conditions, you must first control
yourself.

Napoleon Hill, *Think and Grow Rich*

It is difficult to imagine life before wireless communication. Being just a speed dial away from friends and family
gives a sense of security and convenience not many of us are
willing to give up. It's the big bills we could live without.

More than 90 percent of all American adults now have a cell
phone, and 58 percent of American adults have a smartphone
with a data plan.[1] The average monthly bill with Verizon, the

165

largest wireless provider, is $148 including taxes and fees.[2] But this doesn't mean we've given up our landlines. Nope, for two-thirds of American households, this pricey cell phone phenomenon is in addition to the household telephone bill.[3] Another bill, an additional expense.

So have you looked at your phone bills lately? Maybe it's time to do just that. It's quite possible you can get the costs down to half the price. It's a matter of knowing your options, selecting the best plan, and then exercising personal discipline so as not to exceed your contract limits. That means the kids too—the connected generation.

The Phone at Home

Let's talk about your landline for a moment. I can't believe I'm bringing this up, but given the number of households that still lease their phones from the phone company, may I suggest this is horribly ill-advised?[4] You are paying thousands of dollars for a $25 instrument. If your phone belongs to the phone company, give it back, then follow up to make sure the charge disappears from your phone bill each month. You can buy a cordless home landline phone just about anywhere for $20 or less.

Communication as a whole is a rapidly changing phenomenon. With the advent of voice-over internet protocol (VOIP) and digital phone service through one's cable TV company, it is not reasonable for me to address each and every option, only to suggest that more options are coming down the pike.

But before you dump your traditional landline, consider this. In most areas, the emergency 911 system is tied to your home landline—your traditional telephone number. Giving up this line in favor of using your cell phone exclusively or setting up a VOIP system could jeopardize your safety. When you dial 911 from your landline, your address is available to the operator so emergency services can be immediately dispatched. Calling 911 from a cell phone or other communication source is not universally reliable enough to pinpoint your exact location.

However, by the time I complete this paragraph, that could have all changed, rendering the previous paragraphs hopelessly outdated. So stay on top of what's going on in your area. And above all, compare costs. Do not contract for more service than you require, and be cautious about jumping on the bandwagon just because something is cool. If you don't need something, cool is not reason enough to pay for it.

Long-Distance Calling

At the same time, I want you to consider dumping the long-distance portion of your landline phone service. Your long-distance service plan is likely to be riddled with mystery fees. My experience is that no one really knows what these fees are for (just call customer service and ask—the explanations will be quite amusing), but they add up nonetheless. Try dividing the number of your long-distance minutes last month into the total amount you paid for long-distance calling, including all of those mystery fees. You may choke when you see that your rate is 25 or 35 cents, or even higher, per minute. You can beat that price.

But first, let's get back to kissing your landline long-distance service good-bye. You won't miss it, and you have good and much cheaper alternatives.

First, if you have a cell phone with long-distance service, use it for your long-distance calling. Just make sure you do not go over your allotted minutes or rack up roaming charges. If you have unlimited long-distance calling on the weekends or during off-peak times, don't guess when those times kick in. Call to ask. Check your plan in advance so you know what you are paying each month and what the costs might be for going over.

Next, you need to purchase a prepaid long-distance phone card. This is the key to keeping your long-distance calling cheap. And I mean less than 3 cents a minute to anywhere in the US. The best prepaid phone cards are available at warehouse discount clubs (Costco, Sam's Club, and BJ's). A prepaid phone card is simple to use. You dial a toll-free number and follow the directions. Keep your long-distance card by your phone and you'll never be out of touch, but you will avoid spending a lot of money.

As you appraise long-distance prepaid phone cards, look at the price per minute. Cards you buy in an airport are 50 cents per minute (or more)—a rate that is outrageous.

Wireless

Big bills, lousy coverage, poor customer service. If that sums up your relationship with your wireless service provider, you may be looking to switch companies—especially now that you can take your number with you. But hold the phone! There's a lot to know before you make the big switcheroo to a new contract.

Staying connected with your friends, family, and the world is not cheap. In fact, it costs more than ever if you have a twelve- or twenty-four-month contract. The problem with a contract is that you're locked in. You lose your ability to shop for a better deal. You don't have to sign a two-year exclusive contract with your supermarket, drugstore, dry cleaner, or hair salon. So why do we keep agreeing to sign a contract for telephone services, locking ourselves into high rates and horrific early termination fees if for some reason we need to break the contract?

To remind you just how ridiculous those early termination fees can be, AT&T's regular $150 termination fee soars to $325 if your deal includes a smartphone or tablet. Verizon recently boosted its $175 early termination fee to $350 for advanced devices.

Reasonable Rates without a Contract

A number of mobile service providers use the same networks as the big boys but with cheaper rates and no contracts. They're known as MVNOs, mobile virtual network operators. Think of them as buying mobile minutes in bulk at wholesale rates, then reselling them to individuals like you and me under their own brand names and at rates that are much cheaper than say AT&T or Verizon.

Here are a few of the more well-known MVNOs and the networks they use:

Page Plus Cellular (uses Verizon network)
Straight Talk (uses AT&T network)
PlatinumTel (uses T-Mobile network)
Boost Mobile (uses Sprint network)

Not all MVNOs sell phones and mobile devices. You can assume that those that do not will accept any device that is network compatible.

The cost of a plan with an MVNO is typically half the price of a traditional contract with one of the big service providers. While these companies provide a great service, keep in mind they're small and they are doing all they can to keep their prices low. You won't get the same kind of customer service or technical help as you might with AT&T or Verizon. But what is it worth for you to cut the cost of your cell phone service and data plans by 50 percent?

Unless you are close to or past your termination date, getting out of your contract is not as easy as just saying bye-bye. Your choices are to pay the termination fee (might be worth it if you can cut your monthly costs by half) or find someone to take over your contract. All of the major companies will allow you to transfer your contract to another person. Finding that someone may not be as difficult as you might think. A friend or neighbor who needs service might be willing, or you can list your contract for sale on CellTradeUSA.com for a $19.99 registration fee. When you make a match, transfer that service and port your number to your new service.[5]

You can also attempt to talk your way out of an early termination fee. Make sure you have a good reason (poor service, spotty coverage, dropped calls, inadequate customer service) and present it with determination.

If You Keep Your Contract

Even if you opt to keep or renew a one- or two-year contract, there are things you can do to keep costs down.

Self insure. Are you really paying $10 a month for insurance? Drop it, then be extra careful not to drop your phone or allow it to meet its watery end in the toilet (the most common cell phone mishap).

Use prepaid phone cards for international calls. Even though your service might allow you to call your grandma in Spain, don't dial directly from your cell phone. Instead, get a prepaid phone card that allows international calling. You will slash the cost of those calls. Online providers of prepaid international phone cards include SpeedyPin.com, CallingCards.com, and Pingo.com, all of which are compatible with iPhone, Android, or Blackberry.

Use free mobile directory assistance. Few wireless plans allow for unlimited 411 calls. If yours does not, don't run the risk of paying the big bucks for assistance. Instead, dial 1-800-FREE411 for directory assistance. You'll need to listen to a ten-second commercial, but chill. It's only ten seconds.

Be aware of data usage fees. Unlimited data plans for smartphones are morphing into "tiered" plans that charge for chunks of megabytes per month. While those chunks may be affordable (2 gigabytes for $25, for example), going over can present a huge financial consequence. The solution is to match your plan to your needs and then diligently monitor your usage. You may need to give up streaming videos, gaming, downloading music, excessive texting, and so on—all of which quickly guzzle up those bytes. Set up text alerts that will keep you apprised of where you are with your prepaid plan usage.

Cable or Satellite Television

Want to put a thousand bucks back into your wallet in the coming year? If you're paying around $100 a month for TV, pulling that plug will more than do it and without leaving you high and dry for TV entertainment.

If even the thought of such an extreme measure feels for all the world like losing your favorite binky, I understand. Oh boy, do I.

It's been a while now since we canceled our cable TV service, loaded up the cable box, DVR, and remote control and dropped them off at the local Time Warner office. While I can't say we dialed our monthly entertainment costs back to $0, we did reduce the cost by more than $100 a month.

We used to have basic cable service that included several premium sports packages like ESPN and movie channels. My husband is a sports fanatic, while I approach the level of junkie when it comes to cable news. Now we have local free broadcast channels and access to movies, TV, and sports online as well as an audio feed for cable news channels. We've joined those who see the internet as the new TV. Here are the steps we took that helped us make the leap.

Get an Antenna

If you grew up fiddling with rabbit ears on top of your family's television set to get rid of snow, you may be getting a little creeped out right now. Relax. In today's digital world, with the way digital signals are transmitted, TV reception comes in crystal clear or not at all. All you need is a decent antenna to add to your TV's built-in digital tuner. Depending on how close you live to a station's broadcast tower, you may be able to get by with an indoor antenna. Not that close? You'll probably need an outdoor antenna to get decent reception.

This is really all you need if you are content to watch free television broadcasting. But if you like to watch movies on demand and enjoy all that broadband internet connectivity has to offer, you have lots of options.

172

Get a Box

A broadband connection lets you hook up your television to the internet and stream shows and movies to your TV. If you have a "smart TV," this connectivity is already built in. If not, all you need is a streaming box that sits between your router and your TV that allows you to access specialized internet channels that offer all kinds of TV content. There are dozens of choices ranging in price from about $50 to $400 or more.

The most popular of these devices are Roku and Apple TV. Having used both, I can promise you that Roku is much easier to use and, at about $100 for the model with all the bells and whistles, is quite an amazing piece of genius. You may have a streaming box already if you have a newer game system like Xbox One or Playstation 4. Many Blu-ray players can stream internet channels as well.

Much of the content that comes through these boxes is free, but you'll be watching older shows and movies. If you want newer shows and content (we do), you will need to subscribe to one or more streaming services like Hulu, Netflix, or Amazon. After much consideration, we settled on Netflix ($7.99 a month) because of TV programming for shows such as *Downton Abbey*, and Amazon for movies, which is part of our Amazon Prime membership ($99 a year).

Add a DVR

Now that we have installed an antenna and added a streaming box to provide Netflix and Amazon, we have replaced most of what we had with cable for about $15 a month plus the $35 in up-front cost for the antenna.

I'll be honest. We love to record programs for later viewing so we can skip through the commercials. After all kinds of research and consideration, we've made TiVo our DVR of choice. TiVo is a very user-friendly device. A basic model costs about $150 plus $15 a month for the service. This brings our monthly TV costs to about $30 as opposed to our old cable bill of $130 a month. Yep, that's $1,200 a year we are not spending for TV entertainment.

Many other DVRs do not require a monthly service. The most popular are PrimeDTV, Magnavox, and Brite-View. We are particularly fond of TiVo because it works so well and is easy to use.

Regrets? We've had a few, but we're dealing with them quite well. My husband is still mourning the loss of ESPN. As for my need for cable news, I am subscribing to SiriusXM internet radio, which gives me the audio feed to my favorite cable news shows via my computer headphones for $14.49 a month.

11

Strategies for Big-Ticket Items

Living in debt is nerve-wracking, insomnia-producing, and family-wrecking. Just don't do it. There is nothing you can buy that feels as good as being in debt feels bad.

Ben Stein

It's not every day you face the challenge (perhaps *trauma* is a better word) of buying a refrigerator, tires, carpeting, furnace, roof, or car. Thank goodness for that.

I call these "big-ticket items" not necessarily because they are large in size (although most are) but because they have big price tags—generally $300 and higher.

I'm no fool. I'm certain you anxiously turned to this chapter hoping for the location, internet address, or toll-free phone number of a secret merchant who sells every home appliance, electronic item, brand of furniture, and choice of car for half price. Hey, while you're dreaming, why not throw in college educations and houses too? That would be great!

Of course, if there were such a resource, by now everyone would know about it. Such a vendor would put other merchants out of business, making his half prices the commonly accepted full prices. Soon we'd be right back to where we are now. Suffice it to say, it's not quite that easy.

These major purchases require major consideration if you want to avoid making a major blunder. There's nothing like a hastily signed installment contract to make it seem as if you're living your life for double the price! And how about that moment of angst after the new refrigerator is delivered and you discover that the competition has the same model on sale for $400 less, including free delivery!

Slashing the cost of big-ticket items is about more than avoiding blunders. With the right information and general principles that follow, you can learn to acquire even the big things in your life for half the price.

Anticipate

Contrary to any past experience you may have had with big-ticket items, they should rarely, if ever, catch you by surprise. If they do, more than likely it's due to your failure to anticipate.

As much as you might want to believe that the refrigerator taking its last tortured breath two days before Thanksgiving was a case of bad luck, the truth is that if it is not still under manufacturer's warranty, you should have known. After all, refrigerators do not last forever. Most manufacturers these days, while loathe to admit it, build in obsolescence to their product strategy to reduce the time between repeat purchases. Expect fifteen years on a typical refrigerator if it was manufactured since the early 1980s. Beyond fifteen, you're on borrowed time. Anticipate.

Of course, there may be times you are unable to anticipate a big-ticket purchase. I can't think of one at the moment (I am the eternal optimist, after all), but no one is clairvoyant or infallible. On those rare occasions, you will bless the day you learned the principles of the big-ticket purchase.

Principles of the Big-Ticket Purchase

Follow the Three-Year Rule

If not now, in time you will be in a position to pay for all of your big-ticket items with cash. Until then, the three-year rule should prevail: Only buy a big-ticket item on credit if it has a life expectancy of more than three years, and only finance it for three years or less.

The purpose for the three-year rule is simple. You do not want to be caught in the trap of paying for things long after they've been consumed or have lived their useful lives. Do not finance a big-ticket item for longer than three years. This is the tipping point at which a durable item becomes less valuable than the amount still owed on it. It will be tempting to accept 0 percent interest or low monthly payments for a longer term. But resist. You do not want to string this out past thirty-six months.

Match Quality to Need

It is not always wise to pay more to get the best quality possible—even if you can afford to do so. Though at times you are wise to pay for the most quality you can afford, the secret is to match quality to need and then buy only that amount.

Determining how much quality you need is not always easy. There are many things to consider. For instance, let's say your child needs a costume for a school play. This is a one-time thing. Your need is very small—good enough to last for a dress rehearsal and three performances. You should look for the cheapest possible option that will meet the need. A purchase like a new mattress would be at the other extreme. That's something you want to last for as long as possible—twenty years or more. In this case you want to buy the most quality you can afford. Then take care of it, and it might last for even a few years beyond twenty.

You should always remember that a big-ticket item has two price tags: (1) the cost to purchase it, and (2) the cost to own it (i.e., repair, maintain, insure, fuel, store, and so on).

Do Your Homework

In December 1995, only 14 percent of Americans had access to the internet. By December 2003, two-thirds of Americans had at-home access. By 2004, more people had internet access in their homes than had cable TV. By 2010, 80 percent were fully connected at home, and in 2014, that number reached 87 percent.[1] If you are not on the internet, find the closest library with internet access and learn how to use it. There is no better, simpler, or faster way to research consumer matters than online.

How does the item you're considering rate with the pros? While not the final authority, *Consumer Reports* (Consumer Reports.org) accepts no advertising and therefore can make unbiased assessments of everything consumer related. I suggest you check out their ratings before making a final decision on any type of appliance, electronics, or other big-ticket item. If you do not want to subscribe to this excellent publication, look for it at your local public library. Or you may find an online subscription to ConsumerReports.org more useful, as you will have access to searchable back issues and reports. Their online research process is quite user-friendly.

I was surprised to learn that *Consumer Reports* does not always give its highest rating to the most expensive option. Imagine that—you do not always get what you pay for! Also, I appreciate the way the publication's ratings are broken down to analyze all aspects of the item being tested and rated.

For example, years ago I needed to make an informed decision about a vacuum cleaner. I came this close to buying a high-end model that I'd seen advertised on TV as having received *Consumer Reports*' highest rating. I decided to check for myself and read the full report. Good thing I did. What I didn't learn from the ad was that this particular vacuum scored high in only one area of testing (picking up animal hair) but came in much lower in its overall rating. The highest-priced vacuum failed miserably in removing dust and microbes from carpet. I have no pets, but I have carpeting, and this was important information. I changed my mind and opted for the vacuum that received *Consumer Reports*' overall highest rating. Remarkably, it was not the most expensive model tested.

Consumer Reports is only one avenue of research available on the internet. A site that allows consumers to give their opinions on everything you can imagine, Epinions.com, is also enlightening, as is Amazon.com. At the very least, multitudes of reviews will give you things to consider that you might not have thought about.

It's likely that you will conduct your most practical research for a refrigerator, computer, or other big-ticket item with friends and family. Ask what they love or dislike about an appliance or electronic item. If you've never owned a side-by-side refrigerator, for example, it may come as important news to you that the typical frozen pizza will not fit into the tall-yet-skinny freezer configuration. Neither will a large appetizer tray or jumbo-sized turkey. You may learn that a bottom-freezer configuration typically features a pull-out drawer that makes searching for lost items much easier. Never underestimate the wisdom of someone who has actually owned an item you are considering for purchase.

Start Early

If you are forced to make a snap decision on a big-ticket item, you are not likely to make the best decision. And worse, if it's a matter of urgency, you may be equally unprepared financially. Your decision could result in new debt. When it comes to big-ticket items, you need time. Anticipate when you will need to buy a car; figure out how old your household appliances are. While you want to do everything you can to keep them running, don't let their demise catch you by surprise. The more time you have, the better and more reasoned your decision will be. Time gives you the luxury of waiting for a killer sale. Time gives you the option to change your mind. Time is on your side.

Know the Policies

No matter with whom you do business, you need to ask several key questions before you make a final decision.

1. *What is your price guarantee policy?* Many merchants will match any competitor's price on an item up to a certain amount of time following your purchase. This is crucial and will protect you in the event that you get an item home only to learn that the store across town is offering the same thing at a much lower price.

2. *What is your return policy?* You need to know this before you make a final decision. You never know when you will need to return something for any number of reasons. Can you expect a refund or only store credit? What is the return time period? Store policies vary greatly, so make it your business to learn this information.

3. *What if this item fails during the warranty period?* You need to know whether you will be able to return the item to the store for repair or whether you will have to deal directly with the manufacturer. You need to know if repairs on large items will be performed at your home and if so how to arrange for this. Make it a habit to attach your sales receipt to the owner's manual and warranty. A handy way to file these documents is in a three-ring binder outfitted with plastic sleeve pages. You can slip the entire manual and documentation into a plastic sleeve so it is visible, searchable, and handy.

Compare Prices

A simple, albeit not necessarily exhaustive, way to compare prices on just about anything is to go online to Google Shopping. Type in the specific item and this search robot will list all of the matching references on the internet with current pricing. This search will even pick up items listed on eBay and other online auctions.

While not every store that carries this item will be listed (remember, this engine is searching websites that sell products), in a matter of seconds, you can get a good idea of the range of prices. Now you have enough information to know a good price when you see one. You may need to get on the phone and call a few stores in your area. Ask a salesperson when this item will be on sale. Hopefully, you will find a way to hold off until then.

Make It Last

No matter what price you pay, you can effectively reduce the price when you diligently maintain that big-ticket item and increase the period of time before replacement. Each additional year you get from your refrigerator is another year to save for a new one. Every mile you get out of your car represents a dollar you are not spending in interest to buy another car. Rotate your tires to extend their useful life; service the lawn mower at least once annually; run a gallon of vinegar through the washing machine every few months; turn the mattresses every three months; change the oil in the car as suggested by the manufacturer. Do all you can to get longer life from items that cost a lot to replace.

Home Appliances

There is no need to waste time and gasoline driving from store to store looking for the best price on appliances. You may want to visit one store so you can actually see, touch, and measure the item you are researching. Then visit SalesCircular

.com and click on your state to find what's on sale this week at Best Buy, CompUSA, Kmart, Office Depot, Office Max, Radio Shack, Sears, Staples, Target, Walmart, and select local retailers in your area. This site, which tracks home appliances, electronics, computer hardware, and computer software, is updated weekly and combines the sales circulars of these merchants into a searchable format.

Discount Warehouse Clubs

If you are a member of Costco, Sam's Club, or BJ's, consider that these three discount warehouse clubs often undercut all the competition on appliances, electronics, computer hardware, and computer software. However, they rarely carry a variety of models from the same manufacturer. You can conduct limited research on their respective websites, and you do not have to be a member to search online.

My experience is that *Consumer Reports'* highest-rated items are what you will most likely find at the clubs. You won't find all of Hoover's or Shark's current models of vacuums, but you will, more than likely, find the one that got the nod from *Consumer Reports.* You will also find a limited selection of refrigerators, freezers, washers, and dryers at the clubs. As always, consider your annual membership fee as part of the price when comparing club prices with non-membership stores.

Other Strategies

Floor models. Always consider making an offer on a floor model. It might show some wear, but if you can get the warranty and a big discount on the price, doing so should merit your consideration. It never hurts to ask.

Last year's model. Just like car manufacturers, appliance manufacturers come out with new souped-up models of refrigerators, dishwashers, ranges, microwaves, and washers and dryers with bigger price tags. Usually the only thing different is a bell or whistle. Before agreeing to the current model, ask about last year's model. Since your main concern is price—not resale value—the difference between last year's and the current model should be of little consequence.

Scratch and dent. It happens all the time. A new appliance gets damaged in transit. The worse the damage, the greater the discount. And unless the damage was so severe it affected the operation, the warranty prevails.

If that gouge is on the side of the refrigerator that will not show, or the dent on the washer is of no consequence to you, let them give you an additional 40 percent off to take the problem off their hands. Many retailers have a special location where they send the scratch-and-dent problems, so ask where you can look at these items.

Energy Star. New appliances that consume energy, such as refrigerators, dishwashers, washers, and dryers, are rated by the government as to their energy efficiency. The Energy Star label (EnergyStar.gov) is the government's seal of approval to help consumers identify the most energy-efficient products on the market.

An Energy Star label will tell you how much energy in kilowatt-hours it will take to operate an appliance for a year. This is important because paying less to buy an energy guzzler will cost a lot more in the long run. Remember, the price you pay for an appliance is only the down payment. An older refrigerator you get for free could be far more expensive than buying a new one that is energy efficient.

Furniture

If there's one thing you need to know about buying furniture, it is this: All prices are negotiable, especially on new furniture. I am fairly confident that I can walk into any furniture store, point to any piece, and ask, "Is this your best price?" Without flinching, the salesperson will knock 10 percent off like clockwork.

My philosophy is that if it's that easy to drop a price by 10 percent, just imagine what might happen if I am willing to wait, persist, and walk away if necessary. An excellent tactic is to hand the salesperson a business card and say, "If you need to meet a quota in the next month or two, and you can help me get a better discount on this sofa or tell me when it will be on sale, give me a call." Then walk away. Leave. Go home and wait for the call.

High Point, North Carolina, is known as the furniture capital of the world, and you can buy direct from some furniture manufacturers. If you live in the North Carolina area, you can order and pick up. However, most of these merchants will ship. Many do not charge sales tax when shipping out of state, which may offset the shipping cost. It helps if you know the manufacturer and specific details about the item, including model number and style name. A good place to start if you are interested in getting a quote on buying furniture direct from the manufacturer is HighPointFurnitureSales.com.

We purchased leather family room furniture directly from one manufacturer in High Point. The final cost, including shipping, was just under 50 percent of the price for this same suite at the furniture store in our area. It was a simple transaction and took no longer for delivery than the store quoted (most stores quote six to twelve weeks for delivery). I figure the delivery truck can drive to my house as easily as to a store's warehouse. It was a pleasant and simple transaction. Here are some other sources for furniture.

Thrift stores. There is a huge secondary market of furniture in this country. If you are willing to look, you will eventually find what you need. And you will find great prices. Goodwill and Salvation Army stores are a treasure trove for surprisingly high-quality furniture, provided you are willing to be patient and persistent.

Auction houses. You may have to look around to find a good auction house in your area, but when you do, get ready for some amazing bargains. While it is likely the antiques will go for higher prices, other pieces that are considered used furniture typically can be purchased for rock-bottom prices.

Consignment shops. Furniture is the latest addition to the consignment store craze. Here you will find quality furniture in pristine condition, as well as home furnishings such as silver, china, and linens. Prices in consignment stores will be higher than in thrift stores but still lower than in furniture stores.

Estate sales. If you have the time and the patience, you just might get lucky at an estate sale. Expect to find rooms of furniture offered in sets rather than individual pieces. Typically, those running the sale are not the relatives of the deceased, so don't feel bad about negotiating. It's all business. The people at the sale are simply hired facilitators.

Unfinished kits. If you are willing to do some of the work, you can save a lot on unfinished furniture. Unfinished furniture stores usually offer assembled but unfinished furniture that you can finish yourself. You can also purchase furniture kits that require both assembly and finishing. Now you will save even more. Check ShakerWorkshops.com and Vandykes. com (search "Furniture Kits") to find kits at reasonable prices.

Rental returns. Most stores that rent furniture (I am not advocating renting your furniture because that is such an expensive option) also sell returned pieces. If you're looking for some real steals, check this out. Simply call or go to a furniture rental store to inquire about their sales. Feel free to negotiate. Remember, they are not in the furniture storage business. Furniture that sits on their floor and in their warehouses does not earn money.

Mattresses

If you want to drive yourself nuts, go shopping for a new mattress. You'll hear dozens of theories on coils, fabrics, stuffing, foam density, and warranties. What I know about buying a mattress I learned from the best: insiders now retired from the sleep-product industry.

Be aware of the confusion factor. All of the major brands like Simmons, Serta, and Sealy make decent mattresses, but if you plan to go from one chain store to the next comparing prices, forget it. The major brands use different names for the same mattress in each of the stores, so it is impossible to compare by make and model.

Shop by level. Each company makes "levels" of mattresses: very cheap, decent cheap, good, and best. That's not what they call them, but you can tell the difference by the pricing within each manufacturer's line of products. Expect several models in each price level.

Get your money's worth. You get what you pay for in a mattress. A very cheap mattress is about 10 percent materials (foam, steel, padding) and 90 percent air. A midlevel mattress is about 40 percent materials. A high-quality mattress will be up to 90 percent materials and therefore the heaviest. The more material, the better the product and the higher the price. You can lift a mattress to determine its quality.

Get the right weight. The heavier the sleeper, the heavier by weight you want your mattress. You will do just fine with a lightweight mattress in a guest room that is seldom used or for your fifty-pound child. But for heavy adults, opt for the heaviest mattress you can afford.

Avoid the pillow top. A pillow-top mattress is a normal mattress with a layer of extra padding on top. It will wear out and flatten down long before the actual mattress will begin to show a dent. But it is sewn on permanently. You'll pay an extra hundred bucks for it ($200 if it has a pillow top on both sides). Buy a great mattress pad instead. Pay $40 and throw it away when it mashes down and get a new one. Your mattress will last for many years longer.

Take a nap. Once you've narrowed your selection to two or three, take a nap. Spend at least fifteen minutes on each of the beds you are considering. Comfort is key, so don't make a hasty decision.

Negotiate. At the very least, you should get free delivery and removal of your old mattress.

Trust the clubs. Warehouse clubs like Costco and Sam's Club carry a limited choice of name-brand mattress sets in all sizes. Typically, they're top of the line at cut-rate prices. But you won't have a salesman to consult (perhaps that's a good thing), and you won't be able to take a nap either. However, I can say from personal experience that the clubs make wise choices. Trust them and you'll knock hundreds off your mattress purchase.

Computers

My best advice before buying a computer is to know what you need and then buy up a level or two. Go to various computer websites to educate yourself. Dell, HP, and Apple are only three examples. I can't think of a big-ticket item purchase that requires you to match quality with need more than a computer.

If you are buying a laptop computer, plan on it breaking down. Laptops carried from place to place get beat up in their travels. Technical support, maintenance, and the cost of an extended warranty are key factors when making a decision concerning a portable computer.

Desktop computers have a better reputation for service. We currently have about ten desktop computers and two laptops at Cheapskate Central. During the twenty-three years since I premiered my newsletter Debt-Proof Living, we've purchased no fewer than thirty-five computers. In all that time, only five of our computers ever required service. You guessed it—all laptops.

I use a laptop computer exclusively. To date, I have had thirteen keyboard replacements, the same number of touch-pad replacements, at least a dozen monitor replacements, and more motherboard replacements than I can count. Dell and Apple even replace the keys when I wear off the letters. None of this suggests that Dell or Apple makes an inferior product; I am hard on computers. I expect a lot. I do opt for the best service plan available and pay for the extended warranty on laptops.

In my work, I cannot afford to be without my computer. And when my laptop decides to rebel, a single phone call has a service technician knocking on my door no matter where

I am in my travels, within twenty-four hours in the case of Dell. Or I can walk into any Apple store and get immediate service. I'm a big fan of Dell and Apple for their service.

If you are both diligent and patient, the place to get the best buys on computers and other electronics is GotApex.com. Let me warn you that this site brings new meaning to the term "sense of urgency." Deals come and go quickly. Contributors discover and post great deals and special offers that often add up to nothing short of spectacular. You'll feel that every deal you see is too good to pass up, and because it will expire in the next five minutes, if not sooner, you will feel compelled to buy right now. The secret is to remember why you're there and what you are looking for specifically and then take a deep breath.

Extended Warranties

Recently, I was standing in line in an office supply store. The customer in front of me purchased a $39 calculator. I couldn't help but hear the clerk offer her an extended warranty. The woman hesitated, then they went back and forth a bit. The saleslady was persistent, suggesting it would be expensive to repair this $39 calculator. I had to look the other way and bite my tongue to keep myself from blurting, "Don't do it! Keep your nine bucks!" Clearly, she couldn't read my mind because she went for the bait, swallowed the hook, and the clerk reeled her in.

If you've ever wondered why retailers are so persistent in offering extended warranties, here it is: money. Now there's a real shocker. Extended warranties provide retailers with a whopping 70 percent profit on average as opposed to about 10 percent profit on the product itself.

Extended warranties benefit the company issuing the warranty more than the person buying the warranty. Companies would not sell extended warranties if that were not the case. Such warranties are rarely a good investment because these days most appliances and electronics are dependable.

The Problem

In general, here's the problem with extended warranties: They don't cover the most trouble-prone years of an appliance's life. If that item is going to fail, statistically it is most likely to do so either in the first six months or much later, long after the extended warranty has expired.

The time between six months old and five years old is usually the most trouble-free time or the appliance's "mid-term." Most manufacturers offer a one-year warranty on their appliances to cover any early failures, which in most cases is sufficient. Extended warranties are usually not offered for the entire life of the appliance, only that generally trouble-free mid-term period.

Exceptions

If you know a particular big-ticket item is notorious for failing during the initial three years, an extended warranty may be a wise choice. That is why I purchased extended warranties for both my treadmill and my laptop—both have high failure rates. And I'm glad I did, because both extended warranties have more than paid for themselves by covering big repair bills.

If you have had miserable experiences in the past with appliances breaking down, the peace of mind you'll get with an extended warranty may be well worth the price. But that's a decision you need to make on a case-by-case basis. Just keep in mind that unless it's a treadmill or a laptop, the odds are heavily stacked against you.

Here's an Idea . . .

Instead of buying extended warranties, set up your own repair and maintenance account. Rather than handing your money to the retailers for extended warranties, pay that money to yourself into an account in your name every month. Never miss; never be late. That way if you do need major repairs, you have the money. And if it turns out you never require major repairs (more likely), the extended warranty fund plus interest will be your profit, not the retailers'.

12

Your Dream Ride
for Half the Price

Debt is so ingrained into our culture that most
Americans can't even envision a car without a
payment, a house without a mortgage, a student
without a loan and credit without a card. We've
been sold debt with such repetition and with such
fervor that most folks can't conceive of what it
would be like to have NO payments.

Dave Ramsey

A n automobile is a major purchase. For most, it is second
only to buying a home. It is also the most dreaded of
all consumer purchases and the one most likely to throw a
major kink into your financial plan.

Big car payments can place you in financial jeopardy faster than just about any other consumer acquisition. Many people assume that the only way to buy a car is with a loan. And with cars getting more and more expensive and loan terms expanding to accommodate buyers' needs, the perpetual car payment is becoming a fact of life for many people.

This presents a serious dilemma. In the fourth or fifth year, a car is likely to require repairs but is not yet paid for. Who can afford the big car payment and the repairs too? The conclusion for many is that it's time to get rid of the car, to trade it in for a new model with a new loan for another six years, maybe seven. But since the car is not yet paid off, the shortfall rolls over into the next loan, resulting in an even bigger loan, bigger payments, and more payments.

It's easy to see how this perpetual-car-payment mentality takes over. "What's the use?" is most people's response. "We'll always have a car payment, so we might as well get used to it!" And with two or three cars per household, the cost of transportation turns into a financial nightmare.

The most expensive way to drive a car is to finance a new car and trade it in every two or three years for a newer car. While a 0 percent loan can make this an attractive way to go because the payment is less, the loan quickly becomes greater than the car's market value, which makes the car "unsaleable."

The cheapest way to drive a car is to pay cash for a late model, low-mileage, domestic model. Somewhere between these two extremes lie untold ways to lease or own an automobile, but not many options will afford you the freedom to own a car for half the price. Yet getting to that place is possible, provided you have a plan.

What Not to Do

I received the following letter from one of my newsletter subscribers quite a few years ago, but the principles and lessons to be learned are as relevant as if it came in today's mail.

"After several years of trading our vehicles in and upgrading each time, we now have a gas-guzzling 2003 Chevy Trailblazer. The current market value on this vehicle is $19,510 wholesale (what we could get on a trade-in) and $22,930 retail (if we could sell it to a private party). We owe $33,335 on a 0 percent loan. We pay $156 in gasoline alone each month. My husband doesn't think there is any way we can get out of this. We'd like to replace it with a cheap clunker that will cost less to operate. We have $1,400 in savings, and I'm just wondering if there is a way out of this, or do we just have to dig our heels in until we pay it off? We really regret all the bad choices we made and would be willing to drive something much cheaper."

Perhaps you have already figured out the poor judgment calls Alec and Tina (not their real names) made that landed them in this nearly impossible situation. It started with a brand-new car financed to the hilt. I can only assume that they, like so many, made the mistake of considering only the monthly payment, not the total cost of the vehicle and, specifically, the full amount of the loan. I suspect they agreed to a long-term loan to get the lowest possible monthly payment. Oh, and let us not forget 0 percent interest!

Before that car was paid off, they decided to upgrade (it's easy to get that new-car fever and a case of the "I wants" when you see other vehicles on the road and in the neighbors' driveways or when your family expands), but they had a problem. The not-yet-paid-for car was worth less than the amount they owed on the loan. But they really wanted the bigger, newer, fancier car.

New Cars Cause Fuzzy Thinking

A clever salesperson suggests they can easily drive home in a new car today, provided they can swing a higher payment. Here's where things get fuzzy. Alec and Tina are so enamored with the possibility of having the new car of their dreams for just a bit more each month that they don't fully consider the big picture (they forget to consider higher insurance costs, larger licensing fees, a bigger engine that eats more gas, and a longer-term loan).

Let's say the car they want to trade in has a value of $12,000, but they owe $13,500. The salesman says not to worry; he will pay off their loan so they're free to buy the new one of their dreams. Wow! That's fantastic.

Of course, what Alec and Tina mean by "pay off" isn't exactly what Salesman Sam has in mind. They're thinking "gift"; Sam's talking "rollover," which means adding on the $1,500 shortfall to the new loan, thereby extending their loan period by another year or longer. But it's not even that easy. Because the salesman doesn't clearly disclose how this trade-in will work, Alec and Tina are unaware that in exchange for this gracious offer, Salesman Sam discounts the value of the car they are trading in, which only increases the shortfall.

Unsuspecting customers Alec and Tina are confused by all the numbers, so the salesman mercifully cuts to the chase and says they can drive the new car home today. He names the affordable monthly payment. What they don't realize is how many long years these payments will go on and how difficult it will be to make them. And, of course, depreciation plays a role in all of this, knocking about 20 percent off the car's market value the moment they drive it off the lot.

I learned through further communication that Alec and Tina did this kind of car swapping more than a few times, to the point that they are now $11,000 in the hole. For all practical purposes, they are stuck, even with a 0 percent loan. They have a car they can't sell, big fuel bills they can't afford, and payments of $555 a month for five more years. It's difficult to see how a 0 percent loan did them any good. Still, things could be worse. They could have agreed to this deal with 5 percent or 6 percent interest, which would boost those monthly payments to $629 for another five years. And while I hate to bring up such a negative possibility, if Alec and Tina wreck this car and it is declared a total loss, they will find themselves in a real pickle. Standard collision insurance covers up to the current market value of a car, not the amount owed against it. Without "gap insurance," which specifically addresses this situation and can be pricey, they could find themselves owing $12,000 on a car that has gone to the big junkyard in the sky with no way to replace it but by agreeing to take on yet another auto loan.

There is nothing like a bad car deal to put a major strain on any budget. Multiply that by two bad car deals running simultaneously, and it can look like an impossible situation. Alec and Tina have three possible ways to get out of their bad deal. I'll explain them to you later. But first I want to tell you how I know about all of this through firsthand experience.

One Story Deserves Another

Harold and I leased our first car way back in 1978 after our car was totaled in the middle of the night as we slept while on vacation and far from home. It was a nightmare. We got the insurance check, which was the amount left once the loan was paid. It was nowhere close to what we would need to buy another car.

Believing it was just too risky to buy a used car, and because the money we had wouldn't make much of a down payment on a new one, we looked for other alternatives. Automobile leasing had just come into its own and was all the buzz. The theory was that by leasing, you only pay for as much car as you drive. No down payment requirements, and your monthly payments are much lower. It sounded plausible. To our amazement, it was true. We leased a brand-new station wagon that would have been beyond our reach to buy. The payments were afford-able, and the cash we had on hand covered the origination fees and lease payment for the first month. It was quite painless.

Still, even with our new car, we were in a mess because we needed a second car. We had the clunkiest of all clunkers as a second car, and it had reached the tipping point, where we were sure repairs and maintenance were costing more than it was worth. The idea of the auto lease stuck in our minds. Why not lease another car? We couldn't think of a good reason not to, and so we did. Now we had two brand-new leased cars. It was very nice.

But wait. Before you stop reading and run off to lease a new car, let me tell you the rest of the story.

Many provisions and hidden costs are involved in leasing a car—buried in the fine print. Auto leases include a huge penalty for each mile over the typical fifteen thousand you drive it per year. And leasing a car is really a long-term rental agreement, along with a promise to return the car in exactly the condition you got it—brand-new with absolutely no sign that you've ever driven it or that a kid ever sat in it, let alone launched a few soft drinks onto its fine upholstery. The lease agreement demands that you return the car at the end of the term with no scratches, dents, dings, or bruises; no wear on the upholstery; no stains on the carpet. Impossible? Why, of course. Just show me any three-year-old car in brand-new condition and I'll show you a car that has been sealed in a garage and driven only on Sundays.

At the end of our two leases, we were up against a wall. We had no cash for down payments on two new car purchases; we had no money to buy used clunkers. But there was another problem. An auto lease contains something called "residual value," the amount the car must be worth at the end of the lease, and if it's not, the person leasing the car has to pay the difference. It's like being upside down in a car-loan deal (remember Alec and Tina?).

Then guess what! We found one of those clever salespeople who pulled a rabbit out of his hat and rolled all of the fees, penalties, and shortfalls from both of our leased cars into new leases for two brand-new cars! "And while we're at it, Mr. and Mrs. Hunt, why don't we get you into the cars you really want and will make you look good?"

And so we did, several times, for a total of twenty-two years. What choice did we have? We were always behind the eight ball, never having saved enough money to own our cars. Our lease payments grew and grew to cover all of the rollovers. But oh, did we drive nice cars! We had the original Mazda RX-7; a minivan; various imports, including a BMW; and a Cadillac the size of a yacht, to name just a few.

We finally got off the auto lease treadmill but not without a good deal of effort. During the last year of the last auto I leased, we sold that vehicle and came up with the cash necessary to pay off the lease. I took a huge emotional leap and agreed not to have a car until we could get ourselves back onto firm financial ground. It was difficult at first, but my desire to stop paying $1,000 a month in auto expenses was quite motivating.

When Harold's last auto lease was finally over, we agreed that we would take the cash we had available ($4,000) and buy the best clunker we could find. We settled on a fairly beat-up Chevy El Camino in good running condition. I can't say the interior condition matched. In fact, it was just one step up from disgusting. I cleaned it with disinfectant and polished that car the best I could, and it still looked bad. But it ran and was paid for.

The car was fine. It was my attitude that needed adjustment. I'd had my own car since I was twenty-one. I enjoyed that sense of independence and being in control of the road. And the radio and the seat position. All of it. I didn't mind following my husband to work every day. I felt independent and modern. But all of that changed overnight. Thankfully, our plan was to endure this sharing thing for only a few months.

But something funny happened. I soon discovered the joy of having a driver. I could sleep, read, talk, or do anything I wanted on the commute to and from work. No longer did I have to pump gas, wash a car, manage oil changes, or send in license fees. Our insurance dropped dramatically. Our driveway wasn't crowded. Having just one car simplified our lives.

After two years, we treated the El Camino—by now a classic and quite collectible—to a new interior. We also bought a new engine and new tires. We were getting ready to have it painted when, tragically, it was stolen. In broad daylight, the clunker I loathed was snatched right out from under our noses. Several days later it surfaced, stripped to the bare frame. Gone forever.

Fortunately, we'd been saving money each month in anticipation of buying another car someday. That money together with the insurance proceeds got us a new truck. To this day, we still share one paid-for vehicle—a black Chevy Silverado. It's now thirteen years old, running like a top at 185,000 miles and remarkably still on its original brakes. As I write, we just booked an appointment to have it repainted. Isn't it weird that the paint job is shot but the brakes have 25 percent of useful life to go?

Whether we will ever go back to two cars remains to be seen. But for now, we're still enjoying this amazing vehicle that continues to serve us so well.

It took a great deal of effort, determination, and attitude adjustment to right all the wrongs we committed in the automobile area of our lives, but we did it and so can you.

Rules for Buying a Car for Half the Price

Here are three rules to follow when buying a car:

1. Pay cash. Hang on. I know you may not be able to do that right now. Just be patient and I will teach you how. This principle is so important that I will repeat it: Pay cash for your car.

2. Opt for a late model. Because new cars depreciate so dramatically (20 percent the minute it becomes a used car), your best economic bet is to buy a late-model, previously owned car.

3. Always make payments. I hope that got your attention! On the one hand, I just told you always to pay cash for your cars. And now I am telling you always to make payments. Both principles are true. You must adopt the attitude that as long as you intend to own a car you must anticipate the cost by making monthly payments to yourself. Unlike a home that appreciates, cars depreciate, so you must always anticipate a car's replacement. Anticipate your automobile needs by making car payments to yourself. Now you are always earning interest, not paying it. You make payments even when your car is fully paid for and even when you are fully satisfied with the car you are driving at the time. Why? Remember, cars depreciate and wear out. If you are not always anticipating the next purchase, you will find yourself rubbing elbows with Alec and Tina in the little cubicle outside the manager's office in some new car dealership.

Pay Cash

The method that follows involves a lifestyle change for a while. It's a short-term sacrifice you make to achieve something amazing that few people will ever achieve in their lifetimes: paying cash for a car and perhaps, if you choose, even a brand-new car. Eventually.

Let's say that tomorrow morning your car is destroyed beyond repair. You must have a car, and because you have no money saved, you opt to buy a brand-new car with nothing down. How much can you afford to pay each month for a car payment? Realistically. $200? $350? $600?

Okay, back to reality. Your car isn't destroyed, and you'll keep driving it for a while. But remember the amount you said you could afford to pay for a car payment each month? Open a special savings account somewhere convenient and begin to make that monthly payment into the account. Let's say you can afford to pay $300 a month. Pay $300 to yourself every month. That's right, to you. Be strict with yourself—rigid and unbending! No late payments, no slacking. In the meantime, and as you are making these payments, continue driving the car you have now for one more year, even if it is a real clunker. You can endure anything as long as you have a plan and you know it will end.

Depending on where you've opened this account, you will begin earning interest, albeit a small amount, on the growing balance instead of paying interest on a conventional auto loan. At the end of a year, you will have accumulated $3,600 cash plus interest in your account in the Bank of You. Not bad!

Now sell your clunker. I don't know what you have or what it might be worth, so let's say you can sell it for $2,000. Put that money with the $3,600 and buy the best car you can find for $5,600 cash. By now you've become used to making $300 payments to yourself, so don't stop. It's a habit, and a good one at that.

At the end of another year, sell your current clunker for say $4,800 and put that money together with the $3,600 you saved during the year by making those payments to yourself. Now buy the best used car you can find for your $8,400. Then continue making those payments.

At the end of year three, sell your current car for say $7,800 and together with the $3,600 from your savings buy the best $11,400 car you can find. Your selection of good used cars is getting better each year. You have graduated from clunkers to much more respectable automobiles.

In year four, sell your most recent car for say $11,000, add the $3,600 from savings, and buy a $14,600 used car. By year five, you have at least $17,000 cash to upgrade to an even better car. By year six, you should have at least $20,000 cash to buy a car.

Keep repeating this process once each year—upgrading and paying cash for a better car. As you become more adept, you will lose your fear of buying and selling cars. And imagine your confidence and personal power knowing you are not at the mercy of a salesman, bank, or finance company as you look for a car. You can negotiate because you have plenty of experience.

After five or six years, buying a brand-new car will certainly be an option. But I predict you will pass. Why? Because by this time you will be so good at buying late-model, low-mileage cars for a fraction of the price of a new one that you will scoff at the folly of buying new and feeling that big depreciation hit on the front end. Still, you will have the option to do exactly as I promised: buy a brand-new car with cash. And who knows? You just might. But I guarantee you will be able to drive the car of your dreams for half the price.

Opt for a Late Model

Whether you call it "previously owned," "gently used," or "secondhand," the truth is that every car is used the moment it leaves the lot with its first owner behind the wheel. So when we talk about a used car, we're talking about a large range—from used for a day to used for a decade or longer. It means one mile on the odometer or 100,001 miles. Here's the key to driving a car for half the price: Make sure you are not the first owner. Let someone else take that 20 percent depreciation hit.

Buying a previously owned car can be a lot simpler than buying new if you deal directly with the owner of the used car. You make an offer based on what you are willing to pay, and the seller either accepts or rejects your offer. It's a lot more complicated buying a used car from a dealer.

Many people have an incalculable fear when it comes to buying a used car. It stems from the myth that when you buy a used car, you're just buying someone else's problems or that the only reason a used car is for sale is because it harbors all kinds of monstrous secrets under the hood and is held together with bailing wire. That myth is far from the truth and a completely overblown assessment of the world of used cars.

In these days of 100,000-mile warranties, improved technologies, vehicle history reports, 0 percent offers on new cars, and state lemon laws, there exists a huge secondary market of high-quality, previously used cars. You will be pleasantly surprised at how many cream puffs you'll find from which to choose. And being the all-cash buyer you are soon to become, you will have even greater bargaining power. Your personal confidence will soar.

Here are a few things to keep in mind when searching for a used car.

Many low-mileage used cars are available in your price range. I know this because I hear from buyers like Alec and Tina who on impulse made a bad judgment call. They need to get out of that new-car deal and are willing to do just about anything—including selling at a loss. I advise people to do just that because they are in such an untenable position with huge monthly payments hanging over their heads. So their loss will be your gain.

Nothing is wrong with these cars; people simply got in over their heads with more payment than they could handle. They can't trade them in; they have to sell them. And no matter what their age, these cars are now considered used. If you're flexible about colors and options, used cars are readily available.

Repairs rarely rival payments. Assuming that a used car, because of its potential for repairs, is more costly than a new one is a fallacy, especially if that new car is financed. The same people who insist that they can no longer afford repairs of a couple hundred dollars a month on their current vehicle will sign up for sixty or seventy-two payments of $350 or more on a new one. What these folks are unwilling to see is that the repairs will not be $200 a month every month. Once the problems are fixed, they will have many more months with no repairs at all, allowing them to save toward the purchase of another car. Learn from their mistakes.

You need to banish a fear of the unknown. The problem for many of us is the fear of the unknown and having to rely on others to handle problems. We fear mechanics and emergency breakdowns. I understand all of that, but it's time to lose the fear. Knowledge is power, and power casts out fear. When buying a used car, be willing to learn. You will be rewarded handsomely!

How to Buy a Used Car

When considering a purchase from a car dealer as opposed to a private individual, keep this in mind: Generally, dealers make a much greater profit on a used car than on a new one.

Does that tell you anything? Whether that means dealers typically pay too little on trade-ins or mark them up considerably for sale—or both is more likely—clearly there is room for negotiation. In most cases, lots of room.

Know What You Can Spend

Before you look at buying a car, you must know exactly how much you can afford to spend. If you must finance part of the purchase price, now is the time to address this. What monthly payment can you handle? Keep in mind you will have to pay registration and titling fees, and many states charge use or sales tax. You will also need a down payment in cash.

If you must finance part of the cost (but only if you must, and for this one last time, hear?), keep the payments to twenty-four months if possible, thirty-six only in an unusual circumstance. Don't accept dealer financing on a used car because you will pay far too much in interest and fees.

You want the shortest financing terms possible so you will have plenty of time to begin making payments to yourself for the anticipated replacement of this car. Remember, because cars are constantly wearing out, they can only depreciate.

If you have excellent credit, go online to Capital One Auto Finance (CapitalOne.com) or E-Loan (Eloan.com), apply online, and get approved within the hour. They will mail you a Blank Check, which you'll have the next day. If your credit is not so great, apply through Auto Credit Finders (AutoCreditFinders.com) instead.

Be Prepared

Make a list of the features you need in a car. Match your list to the makes and models of cars that appear to meet your minimum standards. You can find this information for no charge at sites like Edmunds.com and KBB.com (Kelley Blue Book). In your car search, keep your eye on the local classified ads, other similar publications in your community, and sites like AutoTrader.com. Keep your ears open too. You want to be the first to know about a great car for sale.

Have a Reputable Mechanic

You need to find a real, live automobile mechanic you can trust. Ask friends, family, and co-workers. A reputable mechanic will give you a fairly reasonable assessment of the soundness of a car's mechanical parts. Make sure the mechanic has a lift so he can put a car you are considering up on it so he (and you, if you are so inclined) can inspect the body and frame from underneath. You do not want to buy a car that has been in a major wreck, and the only way to know for sure whether a car has been seriously damaged is to look. Unless it was declared a total loss by an insurance company, there may not be a paper trail to alert you to serious damage. A car that has been wrecked to the point the frame was bent or there are visible repairs such as bars welded to hold two pieces together is not a car you want to own.

Ask the mechanic to take it for a test-drive. Look in the trunk for evidence the paint color was changed. Look for water lines that indicate it might have been in a flood. Checking out a potential car with a mechanic may cost you a few bucks, so narrow your search before you bring in a car to be checked. There are so many excellent cars available that you really shouldn't settle for one with major problems.

Get a Car History Report

Every car has a serial number called a VIN (vehicle identification number). You will find this on a metal bar riveted to the dash just inside the windshield on the driver's side. From the moment it's manufactured until that car is finally crushed in a junkyard and sent to be recycled into a new car, there's a paper trail—a history of who has owned it and where it has been registered. As a consumer, you have a right to look at any car's history report for a small fee.

A vehicle's history report will tell you all about the title on the car. If the car was ever in a flood or totaled for any other reason by an insurance company, it will show up as "salvage." That is a word you do not want to see on the title of a car you own.

The history report will also give you an odometer check. If the numbers on the odometer do not add up to the numbers on the report, you know there's been some odometer tampering. The report will show if the vehicle was ever stolen or damaged in a fire. You'll know if it was ever leased, owned by a car rental company, or used as a taxi or police car. All of this information will help you make a good assessment.

More than just interesting, this is information you cannot afford to be without. Access to the internet makes finding out a car's history simple, provided you are willing to pay for a report. You can go to CarFax.com and pull up the history on any automobile if you have the VIN. The cost of the report is $39.99 for one vehicle or about $49.99 for five reports if you are considering several cars and want reports on all of them.

Do a Test-Drive

On a test-drive, you'll do more than just drive a car. You'll give it a thorough inspection. Every car gives you many clues if you pay attention.

The sounds. Drive the car in silence so you can hear any rattle or engine noises.

The doors. Do they open and close properly and line up evenly?

The finish. Are there bumps or dimples in the paint? These could indicate some major body work or "filling" has been performed. Is the paint color inside the trunk or hood the same as on the exterior?

Under the hood. Is the engine clearly new while the car is old? If there's been an engine swap, you want to know the details and reason for the changeover. You want this in writing with evidence of who did the work and what parts were used.

The interior. Look at the carpeting, especially under the seats, the floor mats, and under the dashboard. Look for water damage or substandard care.

How to Buy a New Car

I find it ironic that most people who buy new cars do so because they are broke. I do understand, sadly. I remember what it was like to have no money to buy a used car. And with financing so attractive for new autos, that often appears to be the only alternative.

If you are broke but feel you can afford a hefty new monthly payment, I want to encourage you not to buy new. Surely you have other options (like driving that clunker for another year).

210

Yet, buying a new car is not always a mistake. It is reasonable if (1) you can either buy it with cash or with a fairly short financing period of no longer than three years, and (2) you plan to keep it and care for it meticulously for a long time. A very long time. Only then can you recover the loss on the front end due to depreciation.

The important thing is to know how to buy a new car confidently so you're sure that you've paid the very least for it. That means you need to go to "school" before you show up at the dealership.

Depending on the deal du jour, it's possible to drive out in a brand-new car without making much of a down payment or any at all. Such deals come and go, and at this writing, 0 percent interest offers are showing up again to stimulate new car sales. It's enticing, remarkably easy, and therefore seems advisable. But don't kid yourself. Those nothing-down deals—even with 0 percent interest—have a five- or six-year loan attached. There's nothing like multiplying a monthly payment by sixty or seventy-two to give you a rude awakening. Think Alec and Tina. They are dying under the weight of a 0 percent auto loan.

Your assignment, should you choose to buy a new car, is to know as much as the salesperson does about the car you want to buy. Know the car, the available options, and the actual cost the dealer pays the manufacturer. Never forget that the power of the transaction resides in the party with the money—you.

Know the Facts

Consider the following elements when buying a new car, and in this order of importance.

Price. You must know with certainty how much you are willing to spend. Contrary to what a salesperson may suggest, the monthly payment is not your primary concern. The most important thing you need to know about a car is the full price of that car. Carry a calculator with you and input the monthly payment and multiply it by the number of months in the term. This is the first price tag you must consider.

Cost to operate. Every car has two price tags: (1) the price to purchase the car, and (2) the price to drive it: registration, licensing, insurance, fuel, maintenance, and repairs. This second price tag is often overlooked in the excitement of getting a new car. The salesperson doesn't care about this second price tag, but it should make all the difference in the world to you. Do the research. Contact your insurance agent to find out what it's going to cost to insure the vehicle. Same for the annual registration. What is the anticipated cost to service the vehicle? Does it require high-octane gasoline?

Loan terms. In the event you will be financing this purchase (one day you will be paying all cash, I have faith), the interest rate and loan term come next in order of importance. You will want a favorable rate that will allow you to pay off this auto loan in thirty-six months or less.

Monthly payment. The monthly payment needs to fit comfortably along with all of your other monthly expenses—within 80 percent of your net income. Never allow a salesperson to make the monthly payment your top priority. Keep control of the conversation and situation, never forgetting that the monthly payment, while important, is well down the line in importance.

Resale value. While you want a car that will hold its value, reselling it should not be your top priority. It comes near the bottom of the list.

Color and options. If you have a choice of color, that's fine. Think it would be cool to have an entertainment system built in for the kids or that leather upholstery is easier to maintain than cloth? Okay. But putting options like these any place except at the bottom of your list of priorities is unwise.

Understand the (Somewhat) Meaningless "Dealer's Invoice"

New cars have a sticker in the window with the manufacturer's suggested retail price (MSRP). Of course, this is what the dealer wants you to pay. It is the retail price of the vehicle with the options listed. You never want to pay this price, and you never should.

You may have heard you should pay no more than $100 over "dealer's invoice," the amount the dealer paid the manufacturer for the car. This is also called the "wholesale price." There was a time when the wholesale or dealer's invoice on any given car was difficult if not impossible to discover. But that's changed. This information is readily available at sites like Edmunds.com and others. But this has become somewhat meaningless because dealers and manufacturers have invented new ways to bury fees and charges in the dealer's invoice.

The dealer's invoice fails to reveal financial incentives for the dealer and something called "dealer holdback." This amount can be 2 to 3 percent of the cost of the car, and the manufacturer retains it for a period of time until after the car is sold. If you were to pay $100 over dealer invoice, that dealer would pocket a great deal more than $100. In fact, by the time all of the incentives and holdbacks are taken out of the picture, the true "invoice" amount can be hundreds, even thousands, of dollars below the invoice amount.

Find the Real Number

The secret is to discover the dealer's invoice minus any holdbacks, national dealer incentives, and customer rebates. That is the most important number you need to know.

You can purchase a report with this information from *Consumer Reports* (ConsumerReports.org). Their "New Car Price Report" costs $14 for one vehicle and $12 for each additional vehicle. This detailed report will give you the closest possible number for the actual amount the dealer paid for the car you are interested in buying. Now add the dealer invoice for factory-installed options. Ignore (and always say no to) dealer packs such as undercoating, rustproofing, pin striping, upholstery treating, and other unnecessary items. Subtract any rebates to the dealer or customer (you can learn about current rebates at Carsdirect.com), add the $100, or a reasonable markup, add the destination charge posted on the official sticker, and add state and local tax. Whew! Now you have the magic number for this specific car. And you know the amount you are willing to pay for it.

Let's say the magic number is $19,100. Fix that number in your mind. Engrave it on your frontal lobe. Become a broken record and never allow a salesperson or manager to deter you from what you want—to pay $19,100 for this car.

Follow the Three-Year Rule

If you must finance this new car, make sure you can pay the loan in full within three years (thirty-six months). This

214

is critical. You want at least three years once this loan is paid to continue making the same payments to yourself. This will ensure that you are prepared to repair or replace this car. Don't get caught in the trap of having car payments and repair bills at the same time—or, worse, having no savings to buy this car's eventual replacement. Now you have the option either to keep this car until the wheels fall off (in which case you will still need to keep saving so you have money to replace it because it will have little if any resale value) or to upgrade while it still has value.

Arrange Your Own Financing

Dealer financing is rarely the best way to go. You will do much better if you go to your credit union, bank, or a site like CapitalOne.com so you are prequalified before you even begin to shop for a car.

When financing is not an issue, you can negotiate more aggressively with a salesperson. Don't visit a showroom unless you are prequalified, and never discuss how you're paying until you've negotiated the price.

Know the Best Time to Shop

You want to shop on a day when there are more salespeople than customers. That sets you up to take advantage of the pressure that manufacturers put on dealers and dealers put on salespeople. Dealers work on a calendar month and year. This makes the last day of any month a good time to show up, as well as the last day of the year. And if it happens to be raining or snowing, it's even better. Storms cut down on willing buyers. Arriving near the end of the day puts you at an even better advantage.

Consider Dealership Alternatives

Costco, Sam's Club, and BJ's—as well as credit unions and the Automobile Association of America (AAA)—offer excellent auto sales programs for their members, which is a great way to go if you dread the negotiation process.

The discount clubs have arrangements with local dealerships for no hassle, no haggling pricing, which is about $150 over dealer cost. Members are also entitled to any manufacturer's rebates, incentives, or special financing offers. You can find a participating dealer and the specially trained authorized dealer contact for your specific area at Costco.com. Click on "Auto Sales." As a Costco member, you will meet with a sales supervisor and bypass the negotiating process. You'll be handed an invoice with the Costco member price—a truly simple transaction.

There are also some non-negotiation dealerships referred to as "car stores." They do not have commissioned salespeople, only order takers. The prices of the cars are discounted from the manufacturer's suggested retail price (MSRP) and dealer cost. If you absolutely cannot bear the thought of learning more than a salesperson knows or don't want to negotiate, this arrangement might be a good option. Still, hold firm against add-ons like dealer-installed options or accessories. And never discuss a trade-in until you have set the price.

Back to Our Story

Remember our friends Alec and Tina? Now that we're informed, let's revisit their predicament. They have three choices.

1. Sell the SUV for the best price they can get and then get a signature loan from their bank or credit union for the shortfall

(about $12,000). While not ideal, paying off a $12,000 loan is a lot better than paying off a $33,335 one. In this scenario, they take the $1,400 they have in savings and buy the best clunker they can find to get them by for now. In the meantime, they save each month the difference between the lower payment on the $12,000 loan and the payment they would have been making on the Trailblazer. This money will eventually help them upgrade to a better clunker.

2. Keep the SUV but double up on the payments. If either Alec or Tina can take a part-time job and devote that entire paycheck to making an additional car payment, their SUV will be paid off in two to three years. That increases the likelihood they will drive a paid-for car for quite a few more years. However, once the car is paid for, they need to continue sizable monthly car payments to themselves in anticipation of replacing the Trailblazer.

3. Their third and only remaining option is to keep going with the loan they have, drive defensively, and drive as little as possible. They do not want to face big repair bills while still making huge monthly payments. Avoiding this may be difficult because, face it, five-year-old cars often need repairs. But by changing the oil regularly, driving as few miles as possible, and keeping up with other routine maintenance, Alec and Tina will improve their chances.

The Dreaded Automobile Lease

Leasing an automobile is, in this author's opinion, a stupid way to drive a car. Forget about it. Leasing a car is a restrictive long-term rental. The car is not yours, but you are required to maintain, insure, license, and repair it as if it were.

Lease payments on new cars are not "a lot less" than what the payment would be if you were buying it. And it's not always true that you can get into a lease with nothing down. Read the fine print. It is not atypical for an auto lease to require $2,000 to $3,000 or more up front.

If you are currently in an auto lease, concentrate on doing all you can to keep the vehicle in pristine condition with as few miles as possible (even then, expect to pay some excessive-wear or over-mileage penalties). Discern the earliest time you can terminate the lease. Then ride it out. This information will be found in your lease document under "Early Termination." You might also try selling it privately. If you attempt to trade in a leased vehicle that is still under contract in order to buy a new car, you will lose the maximum amount of money possible. Don't ever think you can walk out ahead on a trade-in. No one ever has. No one ever will.

13

Disaster, Disease, Death, and Other Fun Topics

I've been through some terrible things in my life,
some of which actually happened.

Mark Twain

With the money we've spent on insurance since we married in 1970, Harold and I could have easily paid cash for a summer home. Or a Rolls-Royce.

Our auto insurance tab alone over the decades is stunning. Having insured two sons from learning permits to being on their own, we know a thing or two about paying through the nose for adequate coverage.

It kills me to think we flushed so much money down the drain for all the types of insurance we've carried through the years. Oh, I'm grateful we never had a fire, flood, burglary, or other crisis to trigger a homeowner's insurance claim. I'm relieved that the auto insurance claims we filed over the decades were relatively insignificant in the big scope of things. And I'm happy that despite all the life insurance premiums we paid, I never received a payment as a beneficiary of a life insurance policy. Still, I cringe when I total all the premiums we've paid.

I wouldn't blame you if you find the subject of insurance so boring, complicated, and beyond comprehension that you're tempted to skip this chapter and take a nap. I hear you. But please don't. Like it or not, insurance is one of life's must-haves. If you drive a car, you must have insurance. If you have a dependent family, you must have life insurance. If you have a pulse, you must have health insurance. If you own a mortgage, you must have fire and liability insurance.

You don't have a choice, but insurance should not cost a fortune. You can do some things to keep your premiums low while not compromising the coverage you need. The secret to having insurance is to have just enough—but not too much—and then to pay as little as possible for it.

General Insurance Guidelines

Insure Your Basic Needs

There is nothing righteous about carrying too much insurance or having duplicate coverage. You could easily wind up insurance-poor if you listen to every insurance salesperson and attempt to remove every risk from your life.

Share the Risk

You share the risk with your insurance carrier by accepting a larger deductible. The deductible is the amount of money you agree to pay toward a loss before your insurance kicks in. Increasing your deductible lowers your premium.

File Claims Reluctantly

If you make too many claims—or the wrong kinds of claims—you run the risk of facing increases to your premiums or, worse, having your policies canceled. If that's not bad enough, most insurers these days report claims of their policyholders to big databases. Originally set up to detect and discourage fraud, these secret history files are now being used by insurers to determine coverage and rates.

The way to protect your history and also save money on your premiums is to know when not to file a claim. Don't be too hasty to report a claim if (1) the damage is less than $1,000 and no one was injured, (2) the loss is the result of your negligence, or (3) the damage involves water and/or mold. Take care of the problem yourself to keep from having these incidents place a black eye on your insurance history.

It is far better to carry a higher deductible and file claims rarely than to pay big bucks for a low-deductible policy and then file everything imaginable in an effort to "get your money's worth."

Press for Discounts

There are many discounts for which a person may qualify. For example, a simple spark arrester attached to the top of our chimney lopped $14 off our annual homeowner's premium. In truth, it was a $2.50 piece of window screen to prevent an errant spark from shooting out onto the roof. We discovered the possibility of this discount on our own after reading an article in a consumer magazine. Asking our agent if this was a possibility for us sent him to a big book on a shelf in his office, and sure enough, such a discount was available.

Never assume an insurance agent will volunteer every possible discount for which you are eligible. You have to prod. Ask your agent to peruse the list of discounts available on your auto and homeowner's insurance policies, and then strive to become eligible for them.

Build a Good History

Grab a highlighter because this next concept is important. Maintain good credit and driving records. Your credit score together with your driving record can have a significant bearing on the cost of your health, automobile, and life insurance.

Remember, insurance is all about assessing risk. If you have a low credit score and numerous moving violations and/or accidents on your driving record, you appear to be one who takes unreasonable risks. You may be seen as accident-prone and as reckless with your finances as you are behind the wheel. Many industries see a person's credit report as a character reference. Because these two reports are so important, you need to monitor them yourself.

Know your state's laws with regard to how long speeding tickets, accidents, and other moving violations stay on your record. Do all you can to improve your credit score (MyFico. com has an education feature). Live as though your life were an open book. It is in more ways than you think.

Shop Around

Insurance companies are in fierce competition. Before renewing your policies, make a few phone calls. Other companies will jump at the chance to give you a quote. You gotta shop around!

If you get a lower bid, call your company to report your finding. Give them a chance to keep you. If they are not willing to match or beat that premium, say you'll be making a change. Longevity with a company may earn you discounts in the future, so don't make your decision hastily. But it takes many years of discounts to come close to a significant premium reduction. Here's the bottom line. Do all you can to stay with a company and at the same time force them to be competitive with their rates.

Automobile Insurance

You're just about to make a decision on buying a new car. But before you drive out in a fancy European sports number, call your insurance agent or log on to Edmunds.com to find out what it costs to insure that gem. Also check with the Insurance Institute for Highway Safety (IIHS.org) for the auto's safety ratings and repair statistics. Domestic cars are cheaper to insure because they cost less to repair. Cars that are highly desirable among thieves are more expensive to insure. Your premiums will increase significantly if your car is on law enforcement's list of cars most likely to be stolen.

Keep Premiums Down

As a general rule, you will keep your auto insurance premium down when you choose to drive a domestic, non-luxury, non-sports car. Just another reason perhaps that self-made millionaires, according to *The Millionaire Next Door* by Thomas Stanley and William Danko (Pocket, 1998), drive late-model domestic cars. They are cheaper to buy, cheaper to repair and maintain, and cheaper to insure.

Bone Up on the Law

While laws vary from one state to the next, all fifty states have laws regarding financial responsibility and automobile insurance. Basically, if you drive without insurance, you break the law.

The internet has sites such as Cars.com that list insurance requirements by state.[1] Know yours. Check them against your current policy. If your car is financed, you have little choice in the amount of coverage you must carry because the lender will set the requirements. If you own your car outright, you have more options regarding insurance.

Unless you drive in a carpool or use your car in the course of work (in which case you need additional coverage for your passengers), you likely have no reason to increase your coverage beyond the state's limits. If your car has a market value of $2,500 or less, experts suggest you should consider canceling the collision portion of your policy.

Capitalize on Your Connection to the Military

If you have a connection to the military—even if it's through your father, uncle, a relative by marriage, active or retired—you may be eligible to purchase automobile insurance through USAA Insurance (USAA.com). Let's hope you do qualify, because it will save you a boatload of money.

This is the same member-owned company, in business since the 1920s, that offers banking services to the public through USAA Federal Savings Bank. However—and this is an important clarification—USAA Insurance products are limited to those who can prove they have a qualifying connection to the US military.

Based in San Antonio, Texas, USAA offers insurance for its members in all fifty states. You cannot beat the low prices and high-quality coverage for property and casualty insurance, life insurance, automobile insurance, and disability insurance. USAA customer service is exemplary, as is their attention to time and detail if you should have to file a claim.

Give USAA a call at 800-292-8302 to find out if you meet the eligibility requirements. They will be able to help you make this determination over the phone. Once you are a member of USAA Insurance, you're in for life, even if your military connection retires or dies.

Don't Duplicate

Insurance is expensive enough, so you don't want to inadvertently carry double coverage. If you have homeowner's or renter's insurance, you may not need personal property coverage on your vehicle to cover personal items that may be stolen from your car. If you have AAA road assistance, you don't need a similar kind of towing service on your car's insurance policy. If you have a good health insurance plan, you typically do not need the medical protection offered on your auto insurance policy. But if you do not have health insurance, this coverage would pay your bills if you and your passengers are injured.

Pay Less Frequently

Check your last insurance statements. Are you paying $5 or $10 extra just for the privilege of paying monthly? That might not sound like a lot until you multiply by twelve and then by the number of years you've been making monthly payments. Find out how to drop that fee. If it means you must pay quarterly, semiannually, or even once a year, do it. Even the little stuff adds up.

Be a Good Driver

This goes way beyond simply not putting on makeup or chatting on a handheld mobile phone while driving (don't do either). The secret of good driving is self-discipline and concentration. Defensive driving means sticking to the speed limit, not running red lights, and coming to a complete stop at stop signs. Do these things not just to prevent accidents but to avoid tickets too. Moving violations are increasingly more expensive as cities and counties are more and more strapped for revenue. To add injury to the insult of a $250 ticket, expect your premiums to shoot through the roof; you'll be lucky if your company doesn't cancel you altogether.

Go to Traffic School

If you or anyone listed on your family policy gets a speeding ticket or other moving violation, enroll in a state-approved traffic school if available. In California, an errant driver can attend traffic school once every two or three years, depending on the county. The driver must still pay the ticket, the cost of traffic school, and the cost of missing work if necessary, but once he's completed the required hours, the ticket is removed from his record and is not reported to the insurance company.

As expensive as a ticket and traffic school may be ($300 or more depending on the offense), it's considerably less than the cost of a premium increase. You will have to pay for the ticket anyway. You might as well get the ticket forgiven, if at all possible. Sitting for eight long hours in traffic school is something you will not want to repeat, so that becomes a deterrent for future tickets.

Qualify for Discounts

Nonsmokers typically get discounts on auto insurance. Got a degree? At least one major auto insurer has determined that drivers with a degree are more cautious and therefore less prone to filing a claim. They give a discount for that.

Companies give good student discounts for youthful drivers who stay in school and get good grades. Some states offer defensive driving courses for which insurance companies offer attendees a nice discount. Insure all of your cars with the same company, get a discount. If that company also has your homeowner's insurance, expect a double discount. You may get a discount if your car is outfitted with an ABS braking system or other safety specifications.

In addition, the type of vehicle you buy could greatly affect your premium. A flashy red sports car usually costs more to insure than a midsized sedan. This is also true of vehicles on the most-stolen list.

Increase Your Deductible

The deductible is the amount of money you have to pay before your insurance company begins to pay. According to the Insurance Information Institute, the difference between an automobile insurance premium with a $200 deductible and a $1,000 deductible could be 50 percent or more. You'll pay for minor incidents anyway to protect your insurance history, so you might as well get a discount for that. Raising your deductible to $500 and eventually to $1,000 is wise, provided you have that $1,000 in the event of a catastrophe. And choosing to have a high deductible brings its own reward. You'll be more cautious and less willing to take risks when you know you'll have to come up with that first $1,000.

Drop Collision and Comprehensive

Collision is the part of your auto policy that pays for damage you do to yourself or your own car in an accident. Comprehensive insurance covers damage done by a force other than another car and driver such as hail, fire, flood, flying squirrels, and so on.

If you have a newer car, you are well advised to carry collision and comprehensive with a high deductible. If your car is financed, you have no choice; you must carry collision. However, once your car gets to the age and condition that if mishaps occur you're not likely to get it fixed—opting to replace the car instead—drop the collision and comprehensive coverages. Use the difference in premium to boost your new-car fund.

Shop Around

Once each year, when it's time for your auto insurance to renew, take an hour or so to call several insurance companies or go online. If companies you contact can't beat what you have, you will gain confidence in knowing you've got the best rate. If they can beat your rate, call your current company with the details of the lower quote. If they won't match it, go with the lower rate. But chances are they will match it because they don't want to lose a good customer.

Health Insurance

Health insurance is another of life's must-haves. Be grateful if you have a group plan through your employer. More than likely it is cheaper than any other form of health insurance; however, these days do not assume that to be certain. You must check all your options.

The Affordable Care Act, a fairly new US law, has changed the face of health insurance for Americans. As you consider your health insurance options, check its provisions to make sure you are getting the best possible coverage for your hard-earned money. You can find the law with additional information at hhs.gov/healthcare/rights.

If you are self-employed or work for a company that does not offer a health insurance plan as a benefit, perhaps you've called to get a quote for an individual health insurance policy for you and your family. It's enough to give you a heart attack. But you are taking an intolerable risk if you go without health insurance altogether. While you might believe you are saving money, it's a risk you cannot afford. People without health insurance die sooner because they receive less preventive care and are less likely to detect major diseases early. Medical bills are a factor in one out of five personal bankruptcy filings— the direct cause in one out of ten. You dare not be without health insurance. You can, though, take steps to reduce the cost of health insurance.

Get a High-Deductible Policy

A high-deductible policy ($2,500 or more per person is not out of the question as a last resort), sometimes referred to as "catastrophic insurance," is meant to cover a big health crisis that requires expensive treatments and hospitalization. You'll have to pay for all office visits, prescriptions, and other routine health maintenance, or what insurers consider the little stuff, but for this arrangement, you will get a very affordable premium. This type of coverage also has a hidden benefit. It will entitle you to pay the lower insurer-negotiated discounts with hospitals and doctors. If you have no insurance, many health providers will actually charge you more than the amount an insured person pays for the same procedure.

Fund a Health Savings Account (HSA)

A health savings account is a savings account into which you deposit money on a tax-preferred basis. An HSA allows you to save pretax dollars to pay for the high deductible ($2,500 in the example above) if the need arises and other out-of-pocket medical expenses not covered by your insurance, such as dental and vision care.

Along with an HSA you must purchase (directly or through your employer) a high-deductible health plan that is HSA qualified, one that will cover you should your medical expenses exceed the funds in your HSA. You can learn more about HSAs at HSACenter.com.

Some insurers will offer you the insurance policy and the HSA in one package so you will not have to open a separate account. Other insurers offer just the insurance policy, and you will have to find a bank or other trustee to open your HSA. The two largest trustees for HSAs are MSA Bank (MSAbank.com) and First MSA (FirstMSA.com).

Join the Farm Bureau

You don't have to be a farmer to join the Farm Bureau in your state. Everyone is eligible by paying a nominal annual membership fee. Members are eligible to receive the many benefits and services available, one of which may be health insurance. As an example, residents of California are eligible to join the California Farm Bureau Federation (CFBF.com), which makes them eligible for health insurance through Nationwide (NHPCalifornia.com). To find the Farm Bureau for your state, simply do an internet search for "Farm Bureau" plus your state.

Become a Small Group

In some cases, two people are enough to qualify as a small business "group." Costco (Costco.com), for example, has teamed up with quality insurance carriers in a handful of states (CA, HI, NV, OR, and WA) to offer its executive business members great health plans. Your "group" can enjoy quality health benefits at a group price with competitive rates. At the Costco website, look for "Business Services" then "Health Insurance" for more information and details. The health insurance plan offered by Costco qualifies as a high-deductible plan with which you could pair an HSA.

Join a Trade Association

Depending on your profession and interests, there may be trade groups you are eligible to join that offer group health insurance to its members. For example, the National Small Business Association is for self-employed or small-business owners, and the National Writer's Association (nationalwriters.com) offers medical insurance as a member benefit.

Life Insurance

The secret to cutting the cost of life insurance is to make sure you have the right amount and the right type of policy. If you don't need life insurance, you'll save a bundle simply by getting rid of it. Just because you are alive does not mean you need life insurance.

Determine If You Need It

The purpose of life insurance is to replace your income, should you die, for those who are financially dependent on you. They would include minor children, perhaps a spouse, and possibly elderly parents in the event you now provide for their care and financial support.

Life insurance is not to make someone rich in the event of your sudden demise (in select situations, life insurance is used as an estate planning tool, but this is rare). Life insurance assures that those people who depend on you will not fall into financial peril if your paycheck were to suddenly disappear.

If you are single, your children are grown, your spouse has an independent source of income and would not be thrown into financial ruin without your income, or you are independently wealthy, you most likely do not need life insurance. If you fall into one of these categories and you have life insurance, you may be overinsured, meaning you are paying for something you do not need.

Determine How Much You Need

If you determine that you need life insurance, the general rule of thumb is that you need eight times your gross annual income. That means if you earn $50,000 a year, you should have at least $400,000 in life insurance. Theoretically, this is an amount on which, when invested carefully, your dependents could live without worry for three to four years—the time it would reasonably take for them to get on their feet and on with their lives. That is the purpose of life insurance, not to turn your heirs into wealthy people who will never have to work again.

Understand the Types of Life Insurance

Single-purpose life insurance is called "term insurance." If you die, your beneficiary receives a check for the face value of your insurance policy, called the "death benefit." If you need life insurance, you want to buy only term insurance.

Term insurance is cheap compared to "whole life insurance," which has cash value and combines a death benefit with an investment feature. Whole life insurance is expensive, complicated, and not advised for a person looking to cut the cost of life insurance without sacrificing the benefit.

If you have a multiple-year policy (many life insurance policies have fixed premiums for ten, fifteen, or even twenty years with a guarantee that the rate will not increase during that term), you are not obligated to keep it for that long. Rates for term insurance have dropped remarkably over the past decade, so it is possible to replace your current policy with a new one with a much lower premium. Don't assume that because you're older now insurance will cost more. If you find a better deal, make sure the new policy is in effect before you cancel the older, more-expensive coverage.

Find the Best Rates

Don't assume you have the best rate because you get it through your employer's group provider. In fact, this is usually the most expensive way to buy life insurance because the premiums are based on the people in the group with the highest risks.

A good broker has access to many companies and can find you the best deal. Or you can shop quite conveniently at sites like Insurance.com, Intelliquote.com, and Accuquote.com. Compare all the rates. With some companies, you may qualify as "preferred" or "preferred plus," while other companies see you as having a riskier profile. If you are a member of Sam's Club (SamsClub.com), you may be eligible for rates 20 percent lower than the typical policy. Have a military connection? Don't forget you are eligible for coverage through USAA.

Lock in Coverage

Once you locate the cheapest rate, try to lock it in for a long time, twenty or thirty years. You will then have coverage at that rate for as long as you need the insurance, even if rates increase in the future. However, keep in mind that you are not locked in for the full term. You can leave at will in favor of a better deal you might find in the future.

Homeowner's Insurance

Going without insurance on your home is, in my opinion, simply not an option. At the very least, you need enough insurance to satisfy the requirements of your lender if you have a mortgage. Beyond that, you need some amount of insurance to cover the contents and also liability insurance to protect your financial assets. In addition, some regions of the country require specific disaster-related insurance. Know what is required where you live. You can save money on homeowner's insurance in a number of ways.

Go for the Discounts

I know I am repeating myself, but let me simply remind you to make sure you are getting credit for every possible discount for which you qualify. This keeps more money in your pocket. Anything that reduces your risk of having a claim may be rewarded with lower premiums.

Review Your Policy

I venture to say that most policyholders don't really know what their policy says, what it covers, what it excludes, or the myriad of disclaimers that limit their ability to be compensated in the event of an insured tragedy. Fortunately, companies are making policies more reader-friendly, but don't expect this to be a light summer read. Slog through it—every single paragraph.

Insure Your Home, Not Your Dirt

While your home and its contents are at risk for fire, theft, and other perils, the dirt on which your house sits is not. When deciding how much insurance you need to buy, do not count the value of the land. In some areas, that can be 30 to 50 percent of a home's value.

Increase Your Deductible

Because you are not going to look to your homeowner's insurance for small loses you can handle, there's no sense paying for the ability to do so. Opt for the highest deductible you can cover in the event of a loss. If you have a $500 deductible, your premium should drop by 12 percent. But you'll experience major savings if you can see your way clear to accept a $5,000 deductible—35 percent or more!

Use the Same Company

By placing your homeowner's and your auto insurance with the same company, you will get another discount. The longer you stay with the company without filing a claim, the bigger that discount will be.

Add an Umbrella

Consider adding an additional personal or "umbrella" liability policy to beef up your coverage as a homeowner or renter. Umbrella liability insurance is so named because it acts like an umbrella, sitting on top of your auto and homeowner's liability policies to provide extra protection. (Even if you don't own a home, remember that you still need renter's insurance to cover both your liability and your personal property.)

Use It and Lose It

While this principle holds for every type of insurance, for some reason it is especially egregious with homeowner's insurance. As unfair as it may sound, the best way to get your premium increased—or canceled altogether—is to even appear that you might have a reason to make a claim. This is another reason to carry a very high deductible to cover only the major stuff and then take care of the smaller stuff yourself. Calling your agent to ask if you are covered for water damage or mold could result in a cancelation, even if you do not have a problem or ever file a claim.

Don't Smoke

Nonsmokers get discounts on homeowner's insurance. Most house fires involve cigarettes, so when someone in the home smokes, the likelihood of a fire increases significantly. Smokers put themselves, their families, and their homes at greater risk than nonsmokers.

Improve Your Security

Insurance companies offer handsome discounts to policyholders who go the extra mile with preventive measures. Install deadbolts on all outside doors and automatic security lighting on the outside of your home. A security system may net you an even greater discount. If you're shopping for a system, find out which one(s) will get you the best discount from your insurer. Install smoke and CO^2 detectors and change the batteries every six months religiously.

Know Thy Water Heater

Make sure you know how old your water heater is and its life expectancy (add a couple of years to the warranty period to get a good idea). A rusted-out water heater can result in a flood, especially if it happens when you are out of town. Replacing it before it rusts through is one way to make sure you don't have to file a claim, which is about the best way to keep your premiums as low as possible.

Maintain, Maintain, Maintain

Water lines on washing machines, dishwashers, toilets, and sinks wear out with time. Replace them every couple of years. If you're going to get flooded, it will likely be the result of a hose blowout—when you're not home, of course. Keep your roof in good shape; don't allow faucets to drip or toilets to leak. Live with the same care and conscientiousness you would if you had no insurance. And in the event that big disaster hits, you'll have your opportunity to place a substantial claim.

Finally, opt for an annual premium payment schedule if your company tacks on service fees for collecting more often and review your coverage once a year. You don't want to unwittingly be paying more to insure items you sold years ago.

14

Travel and Family Fun

This is no longer a vacation. It's a quest. It's a quest for fun. I'm gonna have fun, and you're gonna have fun!

Chevy Chase as Clark Griswold in *Vacation*

If you make one mistake in your quest to live your life for less, let it not be the elimination of family fun and entertainment. You need to keep your life in balance and find ways to do the things you love for less money.

I've seen this happen so many times. A person or couple experiences a kind of financial epiphany after reading a book or attending a seminar. We have to stop spending money! The sentiment is certainly sound, provided they mean spending money they do not have. But too many do the equivalent of saying they will never eat again after they've polished off a Thanksgiving Day meal and are so stuffed they cannot move. At the moment, the thought of ever eating again is unimaginable, and the commitment not to eat again is high. But, of course, it's not reality.

People who make a new financial commitment after making too many money mistakes often do the same thing. They make a list of everything now banned from their lives for as long as it takes them to get out of debt. They hang their RDRP (lingo for my Rapid Debt-Repayment Plan, a visual road map for how and when they will be debt-free) on the fridge right next to a list of "no-mores"—no more eating out, movies, trips, clothes, gifts. The list goes on and on.

I understand. Once you make a U-turn on the road to where you are headed (financial trouble) and seek the road to solvency (financial freedom), you get this burst of determination to make double payments, triple if possible. You are so motivated that you think of more and more things to eliminate.

Just like that, these overly zealous folks move from one out-of-balance situation to another. Their new austerity plan lasts slightly longer than the plan never to eat again. Both are unrealistic and unreasonable. They've set themselves up to fail, and so they do.

I've seen thousands of people turn their lives around, get out of debt, and go on to become affluent. And I've seen many try, then quickly fizzle. Those who make it follow a specific plan and stay in balance. They give, they save, and they see some kind of entertainment as essential in their lives even though they are in debt. All these elements provide balance and make the journey doable. Dare I say enjoyable?

This chapter isn't an exhaustive treatment of all the ways you can save on travel or every possible way a family can have fun together. My intention is to stimulate your creative juices and build your confidence by giving you good, solid advice on how to find travel and entertainment for less.

Air Travel

The flight should have been less than three hours. But bad weather forced us to circle high above tornadoes threatening the Dallas–Fort Worth airport for another two hours. Finally, the pilot announced we were heading to Austin before we ran out of fuel.

The people around me began chatting, and conversation turned to how much each of us had paid for our round-trip ticket on this extended flight. Everyone pulled out ticket receipts for a group comparison. The lowest was $188, the highest $876. As I recall, the high fare belonged to my seatmate. Mine was $188.

How can six people occupy identical seats but pay six different amounts? It's something called "fare bases." One airline may have as many as twenty different fare bases (also called "published fares") for each of the seats on any given flight. Clearly, my $188 was at or close to the bottom on that particular flight, while my neighbor's fare was at the top. I booked my flight well in advance and met the requirement at the time to stay over Saturday on this nonrefundable ticket. His ticket may have been purchased at the last minute with a refundable provision.

Here's the important thing to know about airline fares, using my $188 seat as an example. Logically, if everyone in coach with me on that flight had booked their seats when I did, we would all have gotten the $188 fare. But that's not the case. More likely, there were only two $188 seats on that entire flight. But of course that flight could be advertised at the $188 rate followed by lines of fine print about restrictions.

Not only are published fares complicated, but they also constantly change. No wonder I can search six times in one day and come up with six completely different results. But have no fear because there are ways to discover the lowest fare for the trip you wish to take.

It takes time and effort to pay the lowest possible price for your seat under the least restrictive terms and the best conditions. There is no one-stop shopping when it comes to travel. You cannot count on one resource to be the only place you find the lowest fares and the best deals. If there's one area of life that requires serious homework, it's traveling for half the price. But you will be paid handsomely for your time and effort.

Determine the Lowest Published Fare

Every airline has a long list of published fares that change often. Let's use travel between Los Angeles and New York City as an example. Many airlines fly that route, and one airline alone could have twenty different published fares for the seats in coach, each fare with different conditions. And each flight may have only a few seats at the cheapest published fare.

You can search many ways for airfares and get a wide variety of results. But without knowing the lowest published fare so you can compare your results, you'll waste a lot of time. So the first thing you need to discover is the lowest published fare for the route you want to travel. You can search for this fare in two ways—by phone and on the internet.

By Phone

Call the toll-free reservations number of an airline that flies the route you want to travel. Tell the reservations agent you are not sure of the dates you want to fly (even if you have a good idea). Ask the agent to bring up the list of published fares for the route you have in mind and to tell you the cheapest fare and its terms. This is an unusual request, but the information is not confidential. Be friendly and cordial. If the agent is not cooperative, kindly end the call, then call back to speak to someone else.

Once you have identified the lowest published fare, ask the agent to check the dates you wish to fly to see if that fare is available. If you like what you hear, buy it. If not, you now have a valuable bit of information (the lowest published fare) with which to continue your search.

Online

Go to the online travel site Kayak.com. In the box labeled "Compare hundreds of travel sites at once," fill in the "From" and "To" fields. Do not add any dates, even if you know the dates you wish to fly. Now click on "Plus or minus 3 days," then "Find Flights." This will give you a broad range of published fares from many airlines during the coming month. Here's an example at this writing. A round-trip rate between Orange County, California, and Denver, Colorado, is $188 on the low end and $839 on the high end. But alas, just because a published fare of $188 exists for at least one seat on one flight for that route on that airline doesn't mean there's a ticket available at that rate. (Ah, the wild and whacky world of airline ticketing.) But there could be, and that's where the fun begins. Finding it.

Next, click on "Select" to see the flights that have a seat available for the lowest fare. If you find the fare for your dates, book it here or call the airline directly to avoid the booking fee. But keep in mind that you may have stumbled onto a web fare and the agent may not have access to it.

Search for Cheap Seats

ONLINE TRAVEL AGENCIES

The internet allows you to play travel agent at sites like Expedia, Travelocity, and Orbitz. What makes these "travel agencies" and not online search engines is that they actually sell the product. You pay them directly, not the airline. They are paid a commission in the same way a more traditional travel agent is paid.

As you check each of the online agencies, expect different results. One might turn up information the others do not for the same flight. Just keep comparing what you find to the lowest published fare you already found.

One advantage of online agencies is their package deals. Typically, these include a flight, a rental car, and/or a hotel room. These agencies run travel specials all the time. If you are truly flexible and looking to book a vacation, check their last-minute deals. You never know what might surface. But make sure you have your bags packed. They are truly last-minute deals.

If you are booking at the last minute, you might beat the best round-trip price available by booking the same itinerary with a hotel room thrown in. Many times a tour company like Pleasant Holidays will offer a package deal that includes round-trip airfare plus seven nights in a nice hotel. And the price is considerably less than the round-trip ticket purchased alone from the airline. Even if you can't use the hotel room, you'll get the round-trip ticket for much less.

TRAVEL SEARCH ENGINES

Unlike online agencies, which actually help you book airline tickets, search engines just look for online published web fares. These sites are like little robots that run all over cyberspace grabbing fares for your consideration. No robot is perfect, so it's not a bad idea to conduct your search on several engines.

BookingBuddy (BookingBuddy.com) and Mobissimo (Mobissimo.com) allow you to compare all of the results from Expedia, Orbitz, Travelocity, Hotwire, and Priceline. You can also search airlines' websites from BookingBuddy.com.

Every travel search engine has its own unique features and therefore can turn up different results. It takes little effort to run a search on each of them just to confirm you're getting the best rate.

AIRLINE WEBSITES

All airlines have websites where you can search and book online. And they like it when you do because you save them a lot of money. Expect booking bonuses in the form of frequent flyer miles when you book a ticket on the airline's website. The bonus miles will show up in your account once your travel is complete.

Most airline websites provide complete flight schedules as well as schematics for the seating arrangements in their fleet of aircraft. The more you know before you book a flight, the better experience you will have.

PRICELINE

Priceline (Priceline.com) offers a travel option where you name a price you'd be willing to pay to get from point A to point B. Once you name your price, Priceline checks with major airlines to see if they would be willing to sell you a seat for that price.

This may be a good alternative for travelers with time and flexibility. The problem is you must pay for your ticket before you find out specifics (like the time of day you will travel, how many stops you will make, or the length of a layover). Once again, you have a much better chance of getting the price you want if you know the lowest published rate for the itinerary you need. At least you'll know if you're in the ballpark. Priceline will prompt you if you place a bid so low that there's no way it will be accepted. For what it's worth, I ignored their prompt one time and landed the price I offered.

Priceline is a good alternative for last-minute flights. If you are just two or three days out, the airlines are pretty sure how many empty seats they'll have on a specific flight, so selling one for at least something generally makes sense. But the restrictions are formidable.

TICKET CONSOLIDATORS

These companies buy big blocks of tickets from airlines for resale. And they buy them from obscure airlines you've never heard of as well as the biggies. Consolidators (Cheap Tickets.com is one of the recognized names on the internet) are limited in what they can offer because they do not buy tickets on every flight, but they often offer the best deals on international travel. It would be worth your time to check a site like AirlineConsolidators.com and also the Sunday paper for ads on really cheap fares. Again, read the fine print. Know what you must give up in terms of cancellations, changes, and onboard amenities for that dirt-cheap ticket.

DISCOUNT WAREHOUSE CLUBS

All of the big three—Sam's Club, Costco, and BJ's—offer their members vacation packages such as cruises and other travel deals. Check current offerings at their respective websites: SamsClub.com, Costco.com, and BJs.com. Their prices are competitive and typically devoid of many of the fees you would pay when booking through a traditional travel agent or cruise operator.

TRAVEL AGENTS

Think of a travel agent as the place you get a first or second opinion on long trips that have complicated connections, multiple city travel, and especially travel abroad. A travel agent will not likely get you the best deal for short, quick trips.

These days, a travel agent has to be really good at finding great deals to stay in business because the travel industry has greatly reduced the commissions it pays to agents. And because a travel agent is a commissioned salesperson, you can bet you will not hear about any deals that do not pay a commission. Can't say I blame the agent. Still, that is not reason enough for me to pay more through a travel agent than I will to book the fare myself.

FREQUENT FLIER CLUBS

Join every club for every airline you fly. There is no cost to join, and even if you believe you will never fly this particular airline again, who knows? Once you've accumulated enough miles to earn a reward, use them to buy expensive tickets, not fares on deep discount.

One mile is worth about 2 cents, and getting them for free is a good thing. But purposely charging things on a credit card in an effort to earn more miles is really stupid if those charges go on to create debt. Paying 16.99 percent interest each month on dollars for which you earned 2 cents toward a reward ticket makes no sense.

Airline clubs are rapidly changing the rules and benefits of their frequent flyer clubs. Several have already changed from points being awarded for miles flown to dollars spent. Rewards are harder to get because so many flights have been canceled over the years. With every flight being oversold, it's a rare occurrence when there is a seat available in first class for a club member's upgrade. Redeeming reward miles may not be free either. Expect to be charged fees and tax when redeeming frequent flyer points and miles. So be sure you know all of the rules and regulations of every airline club you join.

Use Creative Ticketing

If you are willing to spend the time and get creative, there are clever ways you can save even more money on air travel.

ONE-WAY TRIP

Buying a round-trip ticket even though you need to fly only one way may save you money because typically a one-way ticket is more expensive than a round-trip ticket. Of course, the return portion of the ticket will be lost when you are a no-show, but you spent less money. It's a good idea to call and cancel the return portion of the ticket once you arrive at your destination.

Split Ticketing

Booking an end-to-end combination is a clever way to cut the cost when a nonstop flight is more expensive than a connecting or direct flight. The way to do this is to split your itinerary into two round trips. Then you will have the option to use different airlines to get the best deals on both.

When researching your itinerary through one of the online travel agencies, use the "Multiple Flights" option. For example, instead of inputting Boston as your origin and Honolulu as your destination, select multiple flights to open a third window that will allow you to type in three locations—Boston, San Francisco, and Honolulu. The results will show you the airline(s) that fly this route with connecting services in San Francisco. You could book one ticket on an airline from Boston to San Francisco and then book a second ticket on an airline from San Francisco to Honolulu if doing so is cheaper than booking one ticket on one airline from Boston to Honolulu.

Hotels

Finding bargain rates on overnight accommodations is easier than ever thanks to online travel agencies and sites such as Hotels.com that double as research assistants.

Like airlines, most hotel chains operate excellent websites that allow you to search and book online as well. But following a few guidelines will ensure that you get the best deal possible.

Assess Your Needs

Before booking a hotel, assess your needs. A family on vacation has different needs than a business traveler attending a convention in the heart of a big city. And you may not need a full-service fancy hotel complete with bellhops to tip, valets to tip, room service with added service charges, a dry cleaners, restaurants, and a steep parking fee added onto the daily rate.

Chains like Courtyard, Homewood Suites, Embassy Suites, and Holiday Inn Express (there are many others) offer excellent accommodations without all the add-ons you neither need nor want. These chains do not have bellhops or valets. They do, however, include in the price of the room some kind of small kitchen with a refrigerator and often a stove or microwave, breakfast in the lobby, free parking, high-speed internet, and so on.

Know the Number to Call

Do your research online, but when it comes to actually booking the reservation, do not call the chain's 1-800 central reservations number. You'll be tempted to do this because it is a free call, but don't yield to temptation. Calling that operator who books rooms for hundreds of locations will get you the rack rate. (This term always makes me laugh. What it means is the full price of a hotel room—the price quoted on the company's website. Never pay the rack rate. There is always a discount for which you can qualify.) Don't book a room through the website either. Pay for the call to the exact location's front desk to negotiate your price and book your reservation.

Know the Time to Call

Try not to call during the rush hours of early morning or late evening. Front-desk personnel are up to their eyeballs in guests checking out and checking in. Try 10:00 p.m. after things have settled down. At least one travel expert insists that calling at 4:00 p.m. on a Sunday is the best time to get a great rate. Top management is likely not working on Sunday afternoon, and the front-desk clerks need to book rooms. You are more likely to get a lower rate.

Ask for Discounts

The price of a hotel room is always negotiable. In fact, there could be twenty or more rates for the rooms in a single establishment. There are corporate discounts, family discounts, and discounts to members of organizations like AAA, AARP, and Mobile and Chevron Clubs, just to name a few. Start by asking which discounts might apply. You discovered the rack rate when you visited the company's website, so you know where to start. If you cannot get a rate you like, excuse yourself and call a competitor.

Know Your Add-Ons

The price you are quoted will be for the room itself. Most hotels do not mention the occupancy and sales taxes, which can be excessive. Ask what they will be exactly. Is there an additional charge for parking? Is breakfast included in the rate?

One of the first things you should do when you get to the room is read the phone-call pricing policy. It should be posted close to the telephone. Are local calls free? Is there a charge to dial a toll-free number? This is one of those hidden profit centers for hotels. If you have a cell phone, use it. If you do not have a cell phone, use the pay phone in the hotel lobby (if there is one) along with your prepaid phone card that you carry with you at all times. If local and toll-free calls are free from your room, use your prepaid phone card in your room for all nonlocal calls.

If there's a fully stocked minibar in your room, look out. There could be a $6 soda and an $18 bag of cashews in your future. You can nip this potential problem in the bud by calling the front desk and asking them to empty the minibar. Now you have a refrigerator in which you can keep drinks and food items you purchase from the deli or store down the street.

Rental Cars

If you are not careful, all the money you saved on the airline ticket and overnight accommodations can disappear in the rental car bill. Do not let the thought of renting an automobile throw you into an emotional tailspin. A highly commissioned salesperson sits behind the desk, so remember that everything you hear is geared to getting more of your money out of your wallet and into her pocket. It's a friendly competition, and you need to win this one.

Call Your Insurance Agent

If you know you will be renting a car, call your automobile insurance agent ahead of time. Find out what coverage you have that applies to a rental car. Typically, your collision and liability insurance covers you in any car you drive. Beyond that, ask about something called "loss of use." The rental agent will bring this up, so be prepared. If you wreck the rental and the company hits you with a charge to cover the loss of revenue they suffer while the rental is being repaired, will your insurance pay for this? It should. Make sure your agent reads the policy and tells you for certain one way or the other. Then read it for yourself to verify.

Plan to be badgered about insurance by the rental agency when you reserve the car. If your insurance covers everything, or the credit card you used to secure the rental offers rental car insurance as a perk (many do), be strong. Just say no.

Know the Number to Call

As you did when booking your hotel room, avoid the toll-free numbers. To get the best rate and the best car, call the exact location where you want to pick up the car. And if there's an agency at the airport and another downtown, call both to compare rates. Don't be afraid to ask for an upgrade once a low rate has been offered. Saturday morning is a good time to call if you need a car the following week. Most weekly renters return cars on Friday night, so what appeared to be an empty lot on Friday could show a glut of cars on Saturday.

Beware of Extra Charges

You will be quoted daily rates when you research and eventually book a rental car. But don't get too excited. That is not the true rate, only the base rate. Many things can push that daily rate through the sky, so know what's coming. Be prepared with the right answers to the questions you will be asked.

FUEL CHARGES

Brace yourself for this method of customer fleecing. If you do not return the car filled to the brim with fuel (allow for time to find a cheap station before returning), you run the risk of paying $4 or more a gallon, and they will charge you for a full tank of gas even if you used only a partial tank. It's just too confusing and too expensive to buy fuel from the car rental company. Always opt for returning the car full of gasoline, and then don't forget to do so before you return the car.

Taxes and Fees

Ask ahead of time about taxes and fees. You will be shocked to see the taxes, surcharges, airport fees (even if the rental agency is not located at the airport), city fees, a charge to wash the car, and on and on. Companies do not always disclose these fees, but you want to know what they are before you agree to the rental contract. That original daily rate that was so attractive can double right before your eyes if you are not careful and willing to speak up. Some add-ons are unavoidable (taxes and government-mandated surcharges), but others can be negotiated, like the fee to wash the car or the massive insurance coverage options.

Extra Driver Charges

Many companies will charge you an additional $5 or more a day if you plan to allow a second driver. You dare not say no to this option and then allow someone else to drive the car. Just be aware of this possible charge. Some companies do not charge for an extra driver, so you need to ask up front.

Drop-Off Charges

Returning a car to a location other than the place you picked it up can be expensive. Know exactly what this will be before you choose such an option. As much as hundreds of dollars in drop-off charges can be tacked on, so beware.

ADDITIONAL DAY CHARGES

If you rent a car for one day but lose track of time and return it 24.5 hours later, you may be hit with an additional day's rental charge. Ask about this before you agree to the rental. You want a company that gives a generous grace period of at least an hour and then charges a partial rate per hour thereafter.

Know Where to Look

Visit CarRentalExpress.com, where more than three hundred independent car rental agencies are rated by consumers. At this site, you can also compare the rates of the national agencies.

Travelocity, Hotwire, Expedia, and Priceline are online travel agencies that book car rentals. At Priceline, you can name your own price. Whichever site you use, remember that the price quoted is only the daily rate devoid of all the taxes, fees, and surcharges that will be added.

Often when you book an airline flight through an airline directly, its website, or with an online travel agency, you will be offered an option to add on a rental car or a hotel room. This might be a good deal, but you'll only know if you have done your homework and know how to compare those rates.

Fun on Family Vacations

Family vacations don't have to cost a lot, especially if you find free activities.

Factory Tours

Factory tours can make for great vacation fun, especially when the company manufactures something kids like. Free samples can't hurt! You may not have to travel far to take one of these fun field trips. There may be tours right in your own city.

Here's just a sampling of tours available in different parts of the country.

Mrs. Grossman's, Petaluma, California. This is the sticker company kids and scrapbookers know and love. Mrs. Grossman's prints fifteen thousand miles of stickers every year! Your family can see what's behind the fuss on a free factory tour of the bright and colorful printing plant. The tour begins with a video narrated by the owner's dog Angus and concludes with a free sticker-art class and a gift bag stuffed with stickers. A gift shop sells all of the company's seven hundred sticker designs. Reservations are recommended. Call 800-429-4549 or go to MrsGrossmans.com for details.

Tillamook Cheese, Tillamook, Oregon. Visitors are treated to a free tour showcasing the entire cheese-making process from cow to mouth. Interactive kiosks provide nutritional information for kids of all ages. As visitors reach the end of the tour, they are treated to samples of Tillamook's famous cheese. For more information and tour times, go to TillamookCheese.com.

US Bureau of Engraving and Printing, Fort Worth, Texas. At the Western Currency Facility, adults and kids will love learning all about US paper currency. Best of all, you can see billions of dollars being printed as you walk along an enclosed walkway suspended over the production floor. Before or after your tour, enjoy two floors of interactive exhibits showcasing the history of currency and the intricacies of the printing process. Other features of the visitor center include a theater, a gift shop, and a vending and rest area. The tour and visitor center are free to the public. To schedule a tour, call 866-865-1194 or visit MoneyFactory.com and click on "Locations and Tours."

Dozens of other great factory tours are located in every state. Find a list by state at FactoryToursUSA.com.

Museums

Living history museums. At least two thousand living history museums around the country bring the past to life and offer learning as a joyous adventure. Spring and summer are the best times to visit because they offer many special children's programs and family events. Many can be seen in an afternoon, while others might require an entire weekend. I suggest you start with a virtual visit. Go to ALHfam.org, the site of the Association for Living History Farms and Agricultural Museums, which covers every area of the US and Canada. You can take a virtual tour of wonderful places like the Jamestown Settlement in Williamsburg, Virginia; the Henry Ford Museum in Dearborn, Michigan; and Conner Prairie in Fishers, Indiana, to name just a few. You can find hours of operation, entrance fees, and the programs they currently offer.

Children's museums. There are over 250 children's museums in the US, most of them offering free admission one day each month. The Association of Children's Museums (ChildrensMuseums.org or 202-898-1080) will give you specific information on all of the children's museums in the US, including free days.

Washington, DC. A trip to our nation's capital is interesting, historical, and educational, and the majority of museums and tours around the city are free.

15

Your Satisfaction Guaranteed

Consumers need to know how to write letters of
complaint, petition or appeal, in order to get what
they fairly deserve.

Ellen Phillips,
Shocked, Appalled, and Dismayed!

When you've spent so much time and effort to get the
best price, the last thing you want is to get ripped
off. When that happens, you need to exercise the same level
of care and diligence that got you the great deal in the first
place. Make sure you protect your consumer rights so you
can be fully satisfied with the goods and services you buy. The
law is on your side when it comes to customer satisfaction.

Are you ever frustrated with customer service? Have you ever been cheated, taken to the cleaners, or hung out to dry by a retailer or service provider? Nothing is quite as frustrating as working hard to be a good steward of your money only to discover you are dissatisfied with the purchase. To be a savvy consumer, you need the know-how and the confidence to make sure that, no matter what, no one ever gets your hard-earned money without your permission.

Cheapskate Central is a bustling, busy place. We ship loads of parcels every day, and nearly all of our mail goes by US Postal Service. However, when we have large shipments, we call UPS. Because we don't ship regularly by UPS, we do not have a corporate account. We pay the driver at pickup, something we've done for years.

Some months ago, we began getting annoying past-due notices from UPS. A call to customer service to point out that we have no account and always pay in advance fell on deaf ears. The next notice we got said we'd been turned over to collection for failure to pay two outstanding invoices.

We made copies of our paid receipts and our canceled checks for both of the shipments in question. That did absolutely no good. UPS customer service would not deal with us since they'd turned our situation over to collection. Collection personnel were rude and completely unimpressed with our proof of payment.

After several months of this ridiculous runaround, my staff's collective frustration reached a fever pitch. It was time for me to move into action. I went to the UPS website, clicked on "Investor Relations," and found the names of the top executives and those on the board of directors, complete with titles and corporate mailing address.

I wrote a letter to the president. I began, Dear Sir, I am shocked, appalled, and dismayed . . .

I proceeded to outline our situation and the steps we had taken in an attempt to solve the problem, naming names and giving dates. Next, I told the president specifically the way I wanted this matter resolved and the date by which that needed to happen. I was not rude but assertive and professional. I did not ask for anything unusual or inappropriate. I wanted the matter to be resolved, all negatives removed from our record, and a letter stating that we did not owe UPS any money. I attached copies of the supporting documentation and sent it. I hoped that my displeasure with UPS would be subtly emphasized when my package arrived via FedEx.

Within a week, not only did we receive a personal phone call of apology, but we also received a letter of assurance and evidence that no negative marks were associated with our company. Then UPS went one better. They enclosed a generous check to cover the cost of—you guessed it!—our FedEx charges. I was in a forgiving mood. The matter was settled exactly as I had requested, and we continue to ship by UPS.

When things don't go right with a product or service, you have the right as a customer to expect some kind of adjustment. That might be a refund, a replacement, or an apology. But that's not likely to happen unless you take the initiative.

Making Your Voice Heard

Sometimes you just have to complain! The secret is to do so with such style and grace that your opponent is prompted to act—not out of duress but because you present a compelling

261

case and make it possible for him to remediate the circumstance with dignity and grace.

Keep track of the facts. While the details are fresh in your mind, write down what happened. Include as many details as possible so you don't have to rely on your memory.

Start easy. Make at least one good-faith attempt to reach a resolution at the customer service level. Don't threaten; simply state your case and the resolution you expect. Take notes. Keep a paper trail that includes names of the people you speak with, including their titles and phone numbers.

Be nice. No matter your method of communication, do not make threats or use foul language. Wait until your anger subsides. Stay calm; keep it professional.

Write to the top. If you cannot reasonably resolve the issue, head straight for the top. Don't waste your time working up the ladder. Go to the company's website or call the corporate office to find the name and mailing address of the president.

State your case. Be very clear about what the problem is, what you have done to attempt a resolution, and exactly how you want the situation resolved.

Use strong language. Words like *shocking, appalled, egregious, outraged,* and *reprehensible* get people's attention. Use these words if they fairly describe your situation.

Know what you want. What will make you feel better and relieve the bitter taste you have in your mouth for this company? Explain this to the president in clear and precise terms.

Name the date. Give a specific date two to three weeks hence by which you expect this matter to be resolved. Be sure to follow up if that date comes and goes with no response.

Keep it brief. Don't go on and on for many pages. Get to the point; delete all unnecessary words. Try to keep your letter to a single page. Use exclamation marks and other emphases with extreme caution, if at all. Let your choice of words deliver the tone you desire.

Proofread. Some of us can't see our own spelling and grammatical errors. Find someone willing to proof your finished letter. There's nothing like poor grammar and typos to detract, devalue, and dilute your message. Keep working at it until your letter is impeccable. Now the president will take your matter seriously.

Attach documentation. Make copies of the items that support your claim and prove your situation. Do not send original receipts, claim tickets, or photos. Keep those originals in a safe place.

Say thank you. Assume the best and thank the president in advance for his or her attention and for resolving this matter for you.

Make it easy to respond. Be sure to give the president an easy way to contact you. Give your name, address, phone number, and the best time to reach you.

Be bold. Use bold and capital letters when you type the following in the lower left area of the envelope: FOR IMMEDIATE AND PERSONAL ATTENTION.

Get a signed receipt. You have many options to send your letter. It's best if you select a method that gives you a signed receipt. Certified US Mail with return receipt (available at any post office) is the cheapest option; FedEx or Express Mail will get greater attention.

Expect results. Corporate heads are not happy when they're pulled into customer service issues. And rightly so. It's embarrassing for management to discover their subordinates cannot keep customers happy.

Promise to reconsider. The president's motivation to respond to you is to keep you as a customer, not an enemy who spreads bad reports about the company. State in your letter that this is your desire as well if you receive a positive outcome.

Keep copies. In most cases, contacting the top dog will put an end to your troubles. But just in case you have to take this matter further by lodging a complaint with a federal agency or consumer group or, worse, having to hire an attorney, you will need evidence of your attempts to resolve the issue. You'll have a much easier time if you keep copies of everything.

Go higher if you must. You can file a complaint with the Federal Trade Commission (FTC) against any company. Go to FTC.gov, click on "For Consumers," and then on "File a Complaint." Or file a complaint by phone at 877-382-4357.

Your state's attorney general will likely have a hotline or a toll-free number on the state government's website. Look these up and read the frequently asked questions. You may have the opportunity to make your complaint online if you feel that is appropriate.

Common Complaints

Dry cleaners. The International Fabricare Institute (800-638-2627; IFI.org) has a testing facility and investigates consumer complaints against its members.

Telephone wireless services. The Federal Communications Commission (888-225-5322; FCC.gov) oversees complaints about problems with interstate calling, unauthorized charges, and switching services from one carrier to another.

Insurance. Go to your state's website or call the general information phone number to find the contact information for your state's insurance commissioner. Making a formal complaint will undoubtedly create a stir and give you the attention needed to solve your dispute.

Credit cards. While many agencies police banks and credit card issuers, the Federal Reserve Board (FRB.gov) is the best all-purpose place to start. The FRB is required by law to forward your complaint to the appropriate agency that oversees the issuer of your particular credit card. Prepare for major bureaucratic red tape. Send your written complaint to Federal Reserve Board, Division of Consumer and Community Affairs, 20th Street and Constitution Avenue NW, Washington, DC 20551. Or call the Federal Depository Insurance Corporation (FDIC.gov) toll-free at 877-275-3342.

16

Rules to Live By

Hope is not a strategy. It takes much more than hope to improve your financial situation. You're also going to need support, information, tools, and motivation. In short, positive impact comes only from action.

Michael D. Milner, blogger

I have a quirk, a kind of brain glitch that annoys me to no end. I cannot easily distinguish left from right. My brain locks up and gives me that infamous "404 Page Cannot Be Displayed" message.

Of course, I blame this on Mrs. Sailor. It goes back to that day in first grade when she called on me to answer a simple "left or right?" question. I froze. I did not know the answer. This was not good for a child who feared punishment for even the slightest infraction. Worse, I didn't know how I would ever figure it out. No one else in the class had a problem with left and right. My six-year-old reasoning concluded that the class had learned left from right on a day I was home sick. I would go thirty-five years attributing my problem to a missed lesson.

Imagine my relief the day I learned the whys and wherefores of my personal struggle and a few simple exercises to make things better. If I'd only had the courage to say I didn't understand and to ask for help back then, I might have spared myself a lot of grief.

Perhaps you feel this way when it comes to managing your money. It can't be that difficult because everyone around you seems to handle their money just fine. It's as if you were out sick the day everyone else learned the rules of personal finance.

I have just the relief you need: ten simple rules of personal finance to live by. If you will take them to heart, make them your own, and exercise them daily, I promise they will make things better. You will save yourself a lot of grief.

Ten Simple Rules of Personal Finance

1. *Know where your money goes.*
The act of carefully tracking your spending will give you the power of truth about what's real in your life versus what you imagine. Keep track. Write it down every day. At the end of the month, make a simple analysis. Your spending quite naturally falls into categories. Add up how much you spent on groceries, meal replacements, gasoline, utilities,

clothes, and so on. If you spent it, count it—even if you paid with a check or credit card. It's sometimes frightening to see spending in the big picture. A few dollars here and a couple more there do not give a clear picture of where all the money goes. Seeing it in black and white will empower you to make wiser choices.

2. *Give away 10 percent of your paycheck.*

You have two enemies that will do all they can to make sure you do not live below your means, that you spend all that you have and hope to have. The first is greed. The antidote for greed is giving.

Greed is that voice whispering in your ear that you are entitled to have anything you want. Greed keeps you from being satisfied. Giving away some of your income brings balance to your life. Giving connects you to something greater than yourself; it takes your eyes off your situation. Giving is the tangible expression of gratitude and proves the condition of your heart. Giving easily defeats your enemy called greed.

3. *Save 10 percent of your paycheck.*

Your second financial enemy is fear—fear of poverty, fear of running out of money, fear of losing your job, or any number of money-related fears. The antidote for fear is saving. Diligently save 10 percent of your paycheck—over and above any contributions you are making to retirement plans—always and without fail. This is the way to build a contingency fund equal to six months' income (see my book *Debt-Proof Living* for specifics on how to grow your contingency fund, where to keep it, and when to use it). It will be there to carry you through times when your income stream is cut off. And that will happen sometime in the future. Be prepared.

4. *Tell your money where to go so you won't wonder where it went.*

You receive a finite amount of money. Whatever the amount, it is not enough for you to be foolish. You need to plan your spending. I know that sounds curiously like a budget, and if that word creeps you out, don't use it. Just sit down and have a talk with yourself.

How much do you spend for your house payment or rent? Okay, that's a start. Move on to that big monster called food. How much of your money do you plan to spend on groceries? Meal replacements? Clothes? Gasoline? Insurance? Entertainment? If you've been tracking your spending, you have the exact information you need to decide where next month's money will go. If you haven't started, look at your checkbook, credit card statements, and so on. You're a creature of habit, so you can expect the past to repeat itself unless you say it's time for a change. It's your money, so do yourself a favor and decide how you will spend it. You dare not leave it to chance.

Make a simple plan ahead of time—and then have the personal discipline to follow it. This will make all the difference.

5. *Cap your spending at 80 percent of your paycheck.*

The secret to living below your means is to make a conscious effort to put a cap on your spending. Living on 80 percent of your take-home pay requires discipline, financial maturity, and the effort to find every way possible to pay less than the full price for everything from food to clothes, insurance to transportation.

6. *Do not debt. If you're in it, get out.*

You may find it odd to use the word *debt* as a verb. But it works well to describe the act of paying for something with

270

credit and then allowing the balance to become a revolving balance subject to double-digit interest.

Start with your credit card debt. Create a payback plan. Hang your plan on the refrigerator so you see it often. If you are making only minimum payments, nearly all of it represents profit for your creditors. You need that money—it needs to stay in your life. You need to get out of debt! And you can. But you'll never achieve that until you stop adding to the balances. That's what I mean when I tell you to stop debting.

Get out all of your unsecured debts and line them up so the smallest is at the top. Do whatever you can possibly manage to pay that one off as quickly as possible. Then take that monthly payment and add it to the next debt in line. That's the way to get out of debt fast.

If you could use more intensive help with this, check out my Rapid Debt-Repayment Plan. You can find a free demonstration of how it works at DebtProofLiving.com. The plan in its entirety is in my book *Debt-Proof Living*. It is a remarkable plan, in my humble opinion. Once you see how it works, I predict you will know two things for sure: (1) that you can get out of debt, and (2) exactly how to do it.

7. Buy what you need and want what you have.

Allowing yourself to want what you don't have is a terrible waste of energy. Find contentment in wanting what you do have. When you need something, buy it, and then make the conscious choice to be content. Do not shop mindlessly, wandering around shopping malls hoping to find something.

You cannot have it all, but you can have enough. Trying to have it all only leads to misery, because if you live for having it all, what you have is never enough. Having more and more only leads to dissatisfaction and disappointment. Having enough means choosing when to stop. At that point, one experiences fulfillment and the satisfaction of having enough.

8. *Never confuse saving with spending less.*

When you buy something on sale, you are not "saving" money. You are only spending less. Spending less is a good thing and the whole point of this book. But that is not the same as saving. If you were actually saving money when you bought a $1,200 cashmere coat on sale for $75 (Wow! How did I miss that sale?), you would've stopped at the bank on the way home from the mall and deposited into your savings account the $1,125 you did not spend. Most of the time you are only spending less.

9. *Do not try to impress others.*

When you live to impress others, you allow them to make your decisions for you. The truth is no one really cares. Instead, live by your values of honesty and integrity. And never pay retail.

10. *Above all, anticipate.*

Have you ever forgotten to pay the rent? Probably not. That's because it happens every month. You get used to it. You anticipate when it is due. But how are you with anticipating other expenses—things that don't happen regularly each month? I'm thinking of tires for the car, back-to-school clothes for the kids, a new refrigerator, a big insurance bill, or the cost of a family vacation. Doesn't seem the same, does it? Those kinds of expenses are most likely to throw you off track. The unexpected and irregular expenses catch us off guard and send us running to credit cards for a bailout.

Failure to plan is expensive. Choosing to anticipate is the way to head off the big financial blows because you are buying a commodity more precious than money: time. Time to make decisions and to find the best price. Your goal is to always make that half the price!

Afterword

When our boys were small, they loved to play a game at the arcade called Whac-A-Mole. It's a tabletop affair with plastic gophers hiding out of sight. You get a great big rubber mallet, and when you hit the start button, a gopher pops up. You have to whack it hard to get it to go away, but just as you do, another pops up, so you have to whack that one. Another pops up more rapidly, and soon it's a battle of whacking fast enough and hard enough to get them to go away before another pops up. I cannot think of a better illustration for the way some people manage their money.

They spend all they have, use as much credit as they can find, and then start whacking. Because they're not prepared for the future when something unexpected happens, it's like a gopher popping up. They scramble, looking for what bill can go delinquent for a while so they can whack this emergency or that unexpected expense. But as soon as they do, something else pops up. As soon as it's put down, another pops up, and soon everything is happening so fast there is no way to keep up. It's exhausting.

Cutting your expenses will only give you a heavier mallet. It will not take care of all the "gophers" in your life. You need to get rid of your gophers by saving for the future, paying off debt, and then anticipating your expenses—all of them.

A good money manager has a plan to anticipate irregular and even unexpected expenses. A good money management plan brings balance and sanity to your life. It keeps expenses under control and allows your income to catch up and even exceed the amount of money required to live. Once that happens, you will find yourself in the enviable position of consistently living below your means easily and on purpose.

I'd Rather Have the Money, Bob!

Did you see us? Harold and I were on TV with Bob Barker. Before you run to check your TiVo, I'd better tell you this was a while ago. Try 1971.

We were plucked from the live audience of that old favorite *Truth or Consequences* along with two other couples. Ours was a kind of "newlywed game" stunt. They put the guys in a soundproof booth, and we ladies had to predict how our husbands would answer questions.

Of course we won. And a mighty nice prize it was—$50 and a blender. We already had a blender, so I remember thinking I'd rather have the money. We could have walked away with $85 cash.

To this day, watching Bob on reruns of *The Price Is Right* brings back fond memories. Still, whenever someone wins the showcase with $35,000 of all kinds of stuff to clutter his or her life, I can almost hear what the winner is thinking: I'd rather have the money, Bob! But instead, the winner gets all the stuff and has to pay taxes on the full retail value to boot. We got off easy . . . not much tax due on $50 and a blender.

Every day you should suggest that same thing to yourself— I'd rather have the money!

Let's say you see a great new pair of shoes you simply cannot resist. They're on sale, and it's such a great deal. No matter how you pay for them (cash, credit, check), it's a done deal. You've got the shoes; they've got your money.

Here's where your thinking gets all messed up. Your choices, you believe, are to either (1) have the shoes or (2) not have the shoes. One is a happy outcome, the other negative, or so you believe.

How would your decision change if the salesperson had the shoes in one hand and the $50 in the other? Would you take the shoes or the money? That is exactly the choice you have with every purchase. Either you get the (fill in the blank) or you get the money. Either you buy the shoes or you leave $50 in your bank account.

If you could see your lifetime earnings as one big pile of money and watch how each spending decision diminishes the amount you get to keep, I have a feeling you would take your decisions more seriously. You'd opt to take the money more often than the stuff to clutter your life and in so doing move yourself that much closer to living your life for half the price!

Time to Say Good-Bye

We've come to the end of our journey. My work is done, but yours has just begun. But don't worry; I'm not going anywhere. I want to stick around to encourage you on your quest to live your life for half the price. More than that, I want to hear about your progress and all the discoveries you make for new ways to keep more of your money. Write to me at Mary@everydaycheapskate.com. As you can imagine, I get a lot of mail, and while I cannot promise a response, you can be sure your letter will be read, considered, and thoroughly enjoyed.

For the curious, EverydayCheapskate.com is my daily blog. I'd love for you to go there and subscribe. That way I can show up in your email in-box every weekday morning.

I can't wait to hear from you. Thanks in advance!

Appendix A

I promised to share some of my favorite fast and easy recipes with you, and here they are, in no particular order. Nothing in this appendix will take a lot of time or culinary skill. And of course by now you know the bonus, right? You will save money.

Meals

Blasted Chicken

3½-lb. whole chicken, thawed

salt

pepper

Remove giblets from cavity to be used another time. Rinse the chicken inside and out; set in a baking dish (on a rack if you have one that fits your baking dish), breast side up. Do not tuck in the wings or tie it shut. Sprinkle liberally with salt and pepper all over the outside and inside. Bake at 450° F for 45 minutes. Don't peek or you'll blow the results. Remove and allow the chicken to sit for a few minutes. Cut apart with big kitchen shears or a sharp knife. If your chicken is just slightly larger, bake a few minutes longer. Do not exceed 3¾ pounds or the bird will not cook thoroughly on the inside before the outside turns to charcoal.

The high temperature will sear the bird quickly, and this is the secret to keeping all the juices sealed inside. You may experience splattering and smoke coming from your oven because of the grease that is hitting the sides of the oven and also the fat in the bottom of the baking dish. You can alleviate this somewhat by placing two slices of bread in the bottom of the baking dish under the rack. This will create a kind of sponge and keep the grease from splattering so much.

Sensational Rice

1 c.	raw rice (any type except precooked or Minute Rice)
1	onion
2 T.	vegetable oil
1½ c.	chicken broth
1½ c.	water
½–1 t.	salt
	pepper to taste

While your chicken is blasting (you will be quivering with excitement because this is just so much fun, but do not give in to your urges to open that oven door), remove the outside layers from the onion and chop it into small pieces. Heat the vegetable oil in a skillet and sauté the onion over medium heat until soft.

Add the rice. Continue sautéing until the rice begins to brown, stirring constantly (about 10 minutes). Be careful not to burn it. Quickly add the chicken broth and the water. Add the salt and pepper to taste. Bring to a full rolling boil. Cover, leave on the burner, and turn off the heat. Leave covered for about 20 minutes. Serves 4 to 6. Hint: If you start the rice as soon as you put the chicken in the oven, both will be done at the same time.

Serve blasted chicken and sensational rice with a simple tossed green salad and warm bread. This is a meal sure to please even the pickiest eater. You could fix this meal once a week for the rest of your life and never tire of it, it's that great. It's quick, easy, and healthy. And did I say cheap?

I make this meal to serve six for less than $5, and I do it all the time. (I just checked, and I have seven chickens in my freezer . . . oh, how I love my stockpile.) My family, friends, and office staff think I'm a gourmet genius. Please don't blow my secret.

Quick and Easy Stir-Fry

1 lb.   protein (You can use raw and peeled or canned
and drained shrimp, fresh scallops, boneless
chicken cut into strips, any type of red meat sliced
thin, or cubed tofu. You can even use leftover
chicken or beef—just reduce the cooking time if
the meat is precooked.)

2 T.   soy sauce

1   onion

2 c.   vegetables (You can use any combination of sliced
carrots, celery, scallions, mushrooms, bell pepper,
zucchini, snow peas, and canned water chestnuts
and/or baby corn drained well.)

1 T.   fresh ginger

1 T.   fresh garlic

2 t.   cornstarch

2 T.   cold water or chicken broth

1 c.   stir-fry sauce (found in the Asian supermarket
aisle)

  cooking oil

  steamed rice

Step 1. Set your wok or a heavy skillet on low heat. While it's heating, get your protein ready and place within easy reach of the skillet.

Step 2. Place the protein in a bowl. Pour the soy sauce over the protein. Toss so all the pieces are coated.

Step 3. Cut the onion into about 16 wedges. Set to the side.

Step 4. Cut up the vegetables.

Step 5. Place the onion wedges and vegetables on the counter close to the skillet. Peel and mince the fresh ginger and garlic and place alongside the vegetables.

Step 6. In a small dish, combine the cornstarch with the cold water or chicken broth. Stir until smooth and place close to the other ingredients along with the stir-fry sauce and cooking oil.

Turn the burner to high and turn on the exhaust fan. Quickly pour in 1 tablespoon oil to coat the bottom of the pan. Follow with half the protein. Stir constantly for about 2 minutes. Remove to a plate and stir-fry the remaining half of the protein, removing when done.

Pour another 2 tablespoons oil into the skillet and follow quickly with the onion wedges, all the while leaving the temperature on high. Stir and cook the onion for about 1 minute. Add the minced ginger and garlic and continue to stir. Quickly follow with no more than 1 cup of vegetables and continue to stir-fry. After about 2 minutes, remove these items from the skillet to the protein plate. Continue cooking the vegetables in small batches until done. Do not overcook.

Return all the protein and vegetables to the sizzling hot skillet. Add the stir-fry sauce a little at a time until everything is nicely coated. You don't want this to turn to soup, so go easy. Stir in the cornstarch mixture and continue stirring until the sauce thickens and everything is coated. If it gets too thick, add a little water or chicken broth and continue to stir. You're done! Serve immediately over steamed rice. Serves 4 to 6.

Three Packets and a Moo

1   beef roast (chuck, London broil, round—you name it)

brown gravy dry mix

Italian dressing dry mix

ranch dressing dry mix

1 c.   water

Place beef in a slow cooker (no need to brown). Pour the contents of the three packets over the raw meat. Pour the water over the top. Cover with lid. Cook on low for 8–10 hours for a very large roast, fewer hours if smaller, or on high for 5–6 hours. Check for doneness after 4–5 hours because time will vary depending on the cut of beef, size, and so on.

The regular price of these packets of dry mix is ridiculously high. But they are often on sale, and you'll find coupons for them as well. You know the routine.

Hint: If your slow cooker is large (6- to 7-quart capacity), you can cook a very large roast or two large London broils to serve a big group and have leftovers too. Simply double the packets of dry mix and increase water to 1½ cups.

Optional: Add cut up potatoes and carrots during the last hour of cooking; frozen peas during the last 10 minutes. Expect beautiful, rich, dark brown gravy and the best pot roast ever.

Three Packets and a Cluck

1   whole chicken
    chicken gravy dry mix
    Italian dressing dry mix
    ranch dressing dry mix
1 c.   water

Follow instructions above for the roast. Cooking time may vary, so check for doneness after 3–4 hours.

Three Packets and an Oink

1   pork roast

    pork gravy dry mix

    Italian dressing dry mix

    ranch dressing dry mix

1 c. water

Follow instructions above for the roast. Cooking time may vary, so check for doneness after 3–4 hours.

DESIGNER MUFFINS

Tired of high-fat, high-cost, fast-food breakfasts? I've got a fantastic solution: quick and easy designer muffins. With a little improvising, you can make and serve scrumptious muffins in a variety of flavors to make use of (and use up) ingredients you have on hand. Use this basic muffin recipe to get started, then refer to the variations that follow.

Orange Muffins

1½ c. all-purpose flour

1 t. baking powder

1 t. baking soda

½ c. buttermilk

1 egg

¼ c. honey

2 T. butter

2 T. applesauce

½ c. chopped oranges

In a large bowl, combine the dry ingredients and mix well. In a medium bowl, combine the buttermilk, egg, honey, butter, and applesauce. Mix well. Stir the wet ingredients into the flour mixture. Add the oranges and stir to combine. Lightly coat a 12-cup muffin tin with nonstick spray. Fill muffin cups ¾ full. Bake at 400° F for 12–15 minutes or until a toothpick inserted in the center of a muffin comes out clean. Makes 12 muffins.

Variations

Instead of all-purpose flour, use a combination of flours such as whole-wheat flour or cornmeal. You can also substitute up to ½ cup.cooked rice or bran cereal for an equal amount of flour.

Instead of buttermilk, use low-fat buttermilk, soy milk, regular or nonfat sour cream, whole or skim milk, regular or nonfat plain yogurt, orange juice or apple juice.

Instead of honey, use maple syrup, granulated sugar, brown sugar, molasses, or frozen apple juice concentrate (may increase up to ½ cup if you like a sweeter muffin).

Instead of butter, use reduced calorie butter, oil, or margarine.

Instead of applesauce, use any pureed fruit or nonfat plain yogurt.

Instead of chopped oranges, use chopped apples, mashed bananas, dates, drained and chopped canned fruits, blueberries, raspberries, cranberries, raisins, pumpkin puree, mashed cooked sweet potatoes, shredded carrots or zucchini, nuts, or shredded cheeses. As long as you stay under ½ cup, the wetter ingredients won't throw off the wet-dry balance of the recipe.

Save yourself time and make double or triple batches of your favorite muffins to freeze and reheat later. Bake and cool the muffins, freeze them on a baking sheet, then quickly transfer them to tightly sealed plastic bags. They'll keep frozen for up to two months without losing flavor.

Thaw muffins in the refrigerator overnight, then reheat individually in the microwave on high power until warm.

Muffin Mix

Keep a batch of this dry muffin mix in the pantry and you'll be able to turn out hot, homemade muffins in just 20 minutes flat!

    5 c.   all-purpose flour
    1 c.   whole-wheat flour
 1½ c.   sugar
    1 c.   instant nonfat dry milk powder
   ¼ c.   baking powder
    2 t.   salt
    1 T.   cinnamon
   ½ t.   ground cloves

Combine all ingredients. Store in a container with a tight-fitting lid.

To make muffins: Combine 2 cups mix with ⅔ cup water, 1 slightly beaten egg, and ¼ cup oil. With a fork, mix until dry ingredients are just moistened. Fill paper-lined muffin tins ½ full. Bake at 400° F for 10–15 minutes or until muffins pass the toothpick test.

The muffin mix can be kept in the pantry well sealed for up to 6 months, longer when stored in the refrigerator.

Master Recipes

White Rice

   1 c.   raw rice

   2 T.   oil

  1½ c.   water

Forget the instructions on the back of the bag unless you want scorched or mushy rice. Instead, learn how to make perfect rice every time.

Sauté the rice in the oil in a saucepan over high heat until the kernels are well coated and turn bright white, 3 to 4 minutes, stirring constantly. Add the water. Bring to a rolling boil, stirring just to blend the ingredients. Cover, leave on the burner, and turn the heat to the lowest setting.

Leave undisturbed and covered for 15 minutes (do not peek!). Remove from the burner (still do not peek) and wait for 10 minutes or so while you are getting the rest of the meal on the table. Now remove the lid, fluff with a fork, and season with plenty of salt and pepper to taste.

This recipe multiplies well, but as you increase the rice, you decrease the proportion of water. For example, 2 cups rice with 2¾ cups water. Tip: Make a big batch of rice, allow to cool, then put 1-2 cups into individual zip-type bags. Refrigerate. Now you have future meals partly made and ready to go.

Brown Rice

1½ c.   brown rice (long-, medium-, or short-grain)

2 t.   butter or vegetable oil

½ t.   salt

2⅓ c.   boiling water

Making brown rice is not as simple as white. Brown rice, to be satisfying with its nutty, gutsy flavor and more texture, needs to be slightly sticky and just a bit chewy. The foolproof way to make brown rice is in the oven.

Spread the rice in an 8-inch square baking dish. Add the butter or vegetable oil and salt to the boiling water. Pour over rice. Cover the baking dish tightly with a doubled layer of foil. Bake at 375° F for 1 hour or until tender.

Remove baking dish from oven and uncover. Fluff rice with a fork, then cover dish with a clean kitchen towel. Allow to stand 5 minutes. Uncover and serve immediately. Serves 4 to 6. You can double the recipe and prepare in a 9 x 13 baking dish with no increase in cooking time.

Perfect Pasta

Bring a large, covered pot of water to a boil. Drop in a pound of pasta (more or less, whatever amount you desire). Stir. Replace lid and turn off heat. Do not peek until at least 10 minutes have passed.

Check doneness by eating one piece of pasta. If it sticks to your teeth when you bite into it, return lid to the pot and allow to sit for 5 minutes longer. Check again. It should be done perfectly, not mushy but not too chewy either. Pour into a colander to drain. Rinse with cold water. Once cool, you can put 1-2 cup portions of cooked pasta into zip-type bags and store in the refrigerator if you cook for one or two people, or larger portions for a larger group. Either way you'll have pasta for the week (you should use cooked pasta within a week for optimum flavor and texture).

For a hot dish, simply drop the contents of a bag of pre-boiled pasta into a pot of boiling water to freshen and heat it. After 30 to 60 seconds, pour into colander to drain. You're ready to top with a sauce, toss with butter and Parmesan cheese, or make it any other way you enjoy pasta. Or use it cold in a pasta salad.

Chicken and Beef Broth

Because you will be cooking chicken and ground beef a lot, you are going to end up with a lot of chicken and beef broth or stock. The last thing you want to do is throw it out. But freezing homemade stock in big containers is not good either. Once frozen, it will be useless to you because you won't be able to thaw just the portion you need. The solution: muffin tins.

Whenever you have stock or broth, pour it into muffin tins and freeze. Once frozen, pop out the frozen portions and store them in a large zip-type bag in the freezer. Now you can remove one or two as needed without thawing the entire amount. You can use the stock to make rice, soups, gravies, and sauces. Cooking with homemade broth is so much better than canned broth or even bouillon cubes. Cheaper too.

Master Biscuit Mix

(Compare to Bisquick)

    5 lb.   all-purpose flour

   2½ c.   dry milk

    ¾ c.   double-acting baking powder

    2 T.   cream of tartar

    3 T.   salt

    ½ c.   sugar

   4⅔ c.   solid vegetable shortening
            (2 lb.)

Sift dry ingredients together. Cut in shortening until mix looks like cornmeal. Store in a container with a tight-fitting lid at room temperature for up to 6 months. Makes 30 cups.

Biscuits

    3 c.   master mix

    ¾ c.   water

Blend and knead a few strokes. Roll out and cut biscuits with a round biscuit cutter or into squares or diamond shapes. Bake at 450° F for 10 minutes. Makes 12 biscuits.

Dumplings

    3 c.   master mix

    ¾ c.   water

Blend and drop into hot liquid of choice. Cook 10 minutes uncovered and an additional 10 minutes covered.

Muffins

    3 c.   master mix

    ½ c.   sugar

    1   egg

    1 c.   water

Combine water and egg; add dry ingredients. Add optional items such as blueberries, chocolate chips, nuts, and so forth as desired. Fill paper-lined muffin tins ½ full. Bake at 450° F for 25 minutes. Makes 12 muffins.

Drop Cookies

    3 c.   master mix
    1 c.   sugar
      1   egg
    ⅓ c.   water
    1 t.   vanilla
    ½ c.   nuts or chocolate chips

Combine first five ingredients and then stir in nuts or chocolate chips. Drop onto cookie sheet and bake at 375° F for
10–12 minutes. Makes 4 dozen cookies.

Coffee Cake

    3 c.   master mix
    ½ c.   sugar
      1   egg
    ⅔ c.   water

Combine all ingredients and pour into a greased 9-inch
round cake pan. Cover with topping: ½ cup brown sugar,
3 tablespoons butter, ½ teaspoon cinnamon. Optional: Add
½ cup nuts or raisins to the topping mix. Bake at 400° F
for 25 minutes.

Pancakes

3 c. master mix

1½ c. water

1 egg

Combine all ingredients until barely incorporated. Prepare pancakes or waffles as usual. Makes 18 medium pancakes.

Gingerbread

2 c. master mix

¼ c. sugar

1 egg

½ c. water

½ c. molasses

½ t. cinnamon

½ t. ginger

½ t. ground cloves

Beat egg together with the water and molasses. Mix well with dry ingredients until all are incorporated. Pour into a greased 8-inch square cake pan. Bake at 350° F for 40 minutes.

Cornbread

1¼ c.   master mix

¾ c.   cornmeal

1   egg

1 T.   sugar

½ c.   water

Combine all ingredients until fully incorporated. Pour into a greased 8-inch square cake pan or muffin tins. Bake at 400° F for 25 minutes.

Shortcake

2 c.   master mix

2 T.   sugar

½ c.   water

Combine all ingredients and bake in a greased 8-inch square cake pan or roll out and cut into individual cakes to be placed on a cookie sheet. Bake at 400° F for 25 minutes or a few minutes less for individual shortcakes, until they just begin to brown.

Note: You can use master mix in any recipe calling for Bisquick, making sure you substitute water for milk if the recipe calls for milk.

Cake Mix Cookies

You can make cookies from any flavor of boxed cake mix. Just add ½ cup oil, 2 eggs, 1 tablespoon water, and 1-2 teaspoons of any flavor of extract to the dry mix. Mix well with an electric mixer, roll into 1-inch balls, flatten onto an ungreased cookie sheet, and bake at 350° F for 8-10 minutes.

Get creative with flavor choices. For example, 2 teaspoons lemon extract added to a yellow cake mix makes lemon cookies. When cooled, dust them with powdered sugar. Or add 2 teaspoons vanilla extract to a white cake mix for a delicious sugar cookie. How about 2 teaspoons mint extract and a chocolate cake mix? Add white chocolate chips to a strawberry cake mix for a unique result. This cookie dough, once mixed, can be frozen for baking later. Just roll into a log and cover tightly with plastic wrap to freeze. Then slice what you need and bake.

Ground Beef

Once I made a terrible mistake. I froze 10 pounds of ground beef. That big block of frozen hamburger languished in my freezer for what seemed like years. What was I thinking? I should have browned it first, then frozen it in usable portions. But browning beef is such a messy job!

Just when I knew I would never make that same mistake again, I came upon another cheap ground beef opportunity. The expiration date was nearing, and my supermarket needed to get rid of ground beef. Ten pounds! I almost walked by. Then I decided to try something different, albeit a little weird.

I put the entire 10 pounds of raw ground beef into my big stock pot. I added enough water to cover it and set it over high heat to come to a boil, no cover, no salt. After about 5 minutes, I gave it a stir to break up the big clumps, which were few. The hot water was doing all of the work for me—no splatters, no mess. When all of the pink color disappeared, I knew it was done, even though it had not reached a rolling boil.

I placed my large colander into a big bowl in the sink and poured the now cooked beef into the colander to drain off the fat. I put the beef broth in the refrigerator. Later, I skimmed off the fat and poured the beef broth into muffin tins and placed them in the freezer. After the broth was frozen, I placed these individual portions of frozen broth into a zip-type bag and stored them in the freezer.

I measured about 1 ½ cups of cooked beef (the equivalent of about 1 pound of raw ground beef) into gallon-size zip-type freezer bags. I laid each one on the counter to flatten it thin, then stacked them like sheets of paper and popped the stack into the freezer.

Because my bags of beef are so flat, I can use them frozen—no thawing required. I take one of the frozen packages of ground beef from the freezer, whack it on the side of the sink to break the meat into pieces, unzip, and pour the contents into a nonstick skillet. It's ready for all uses. Here's the best part. This method removes the fat, leaving the ground meat virtually fat-free.

CREATE YOUR OWN
DESIGNER CUISINE

Ever feel like a kitchen klutz? Wish you could take that odd assortment of stuff in the pantry, refrigerator, and freezer and make something delicious without a specific recipe and without having to run to the market? Well, grab your whisk and shout for joy! Thanks to this foolproof, five-step plan, you can create fabulous, original, homemade, delicious, and nutritious entrees designed by you using the items you have on hand.

Step 1: Combine 1 8-ounce carton sour cream, 1 cup milk, 1 cup water, 1 teaspoon salt, and 1 teaspoon pepper with one item from group A (omit sour cream and milk when using tomatoes).

Step 2: Stir in one item from each of groups B, C, D, and E.

Step 3: Spoon mixture into a lightly greased 9 x 13 baking dish.

Step 4: Sprinkle with one or two choices from group F.
Step 5: Cover and bake at 350° F for 1 hour and 10 minutes.
Uncover and bake 10 additional minutes. Makes 6 servings.

Group A

1 10¾-oz. can	cream of mushroom soup, undiluted
1 10¾-oz. can	cream of celery soup, undiluted
1 10¾-oz. can	cheddar cheese soup, undiluted
1 10¾-oz. can	cream of chicken soup, undiluted
2 14½-oz. cans	Italian-style diced tomatoes, undrained

Group B

2 6-oz. cans	solid white tuna, drained and flaked
2 c.	chopped cooked chicken
2 c.	chopped cooked ham
2 c.	chopped cooked turkey
1 lb.	ground beef, browned and drained

Group C

2 c. uncooked elbow macaroni

1 c. uncooked rice

4 c. uncooked wide egg noodles

3 c. uncooked medium pasta shells

Group D

1 10-oz. package frozen chopped spinach, thawed and drained

1 10-oz. package frozen cut broccoli

1 10-oz. package frozen Italian green beans

1 10-oz. package frozen pea pods

1 10-oz. package frozen whole kernel corn

1 16-oz. package frozen sliced yellow squash

Group E

1 3-oz. can	sliced mushrooms, drained
¼ c.	sliced ripe olives
¼ c.	chopped bell pepper
¼ c.	chopped onion
¼ c.	chopped celery
2 cloves	garlic, minced
1 4½-oz. can	chopped green chilies
1 1¼-oz. envelope	taco seasoning mix

Group F

½ c.	shredded mozzarella cheese
½ c.	shredded Swiss cheese
½ c.	grated Parmesan cheese
½ c.	fine, dry bread crumbs

Sample Combinations

Chicken Casserole. Cream of chicken soup, chicken, rice, broccoli, Parmesan cheese, and bread crumbs.

Ham Casserole. Cream of celery soup, ham, wide egg noodles, Italian green beans, garlic, and two portions Swiss cheese.

Turkey Casserole. Italian-style diced tomatoes, turkey, medium pasta shells, spinach, onion, garlic, mozzarella cheese, and bread crumbs.

Vegetarian Casserole. Italian-style diced tomatoes, rice, yellow squash, olives, four portions celery, four portions bell pepper, garlic, Parmesan cheese, and bread crumbs.

Now it's your turn. Enjoy!

Make Your Own Mixes

They're convenient and tasty, but have you ever considered the high cost of your favorite prepared mixes and spices? In less time than it takes you to run to the market to pick up a box of Rice-a-Roni or Shake 'N Bake, you can make it yourself and save a bundle in the process. It's difficult to say for sure what these recipes will cost by comparison because there are so many variables, but I can assure you it's pennies, not dollars!

Beef Gravy Mix

1⅓ c.   nonfat powdered milk

¾ c.   instant flour (like Wondra or Shake & Blend)

3 T.   beef bouillon granules

⅛ t.   ground thyme

¼ t.   onion powder

⅛ t.   sage

½ c.   butter or margarine, room temperature

3 T.   brown sauce for gravy (like Kitchen Bouquet)

Combine powdered milk, flour, bouillon granules, thyme, onion powder, and sage. Use a pastry blender or two knives to cut in butter or margarine until evenly distributed. Drizzle brown sauce over mixture. Stir with a wire whisk until blended. Spoon into a container with a tight-fitting lid. Label with date and contents. Store in refrigerator. Use within 4-6 weeks. Makes about 2⅔ cups beef gravy mix.

To make gravy: Pour 1 cup cold water into a saucepan. Use a whisk to stir ½ cup beef gravy mix into water. Stir constantly over medium heat until gravy is smooth and slightly thickened, 2-3 minutes. Makes about 1 cup gravy.

Chicken Gravy Mix

1⅓ c.   powdered milk

¾ c.   instant flour (like Wondra or Shake & Blend)

3 T.   chicken bouillon granules

¼ t.   sage or poultry seasoning

¼ t.   onion powder

312

⅛ t.   black pepper

½ c.   salted butter or margarine, room temperature

Combine powdered milk, flour, bouillon granules, sage or poultry seasoning, onion powder, and black pepper. Use a pastry blender or two knives to cut in butter or margarine until evenly distributed. Spoon into a container with a tight-fitting lid. Label with date and contents. Store in refrigerator. Use within 4–6 weeks. Makes about 2⅔ cups chicken gravy mix.

To make gravy: Pour 1 cup cold water into a saucepan. Use a whisk to stir ½ cup chicken gravy mix into water. Stir constantly over medium heat until gravy is smooth and slightly thickened, 2–3 minutes. Makes about 1 cup gravy.

Country Gravy Mix

1 c.   all-purpose flour

2 t.   garlic salt

1 t.   paprika

1 t.   ground black pepper

¼ t.   poultry seasoning

½ t.   salt

Combine all ingredients. Store in a container with a tight-fitting lid. The best country gravy is made in a skillet with drippings that remain after frying chicken or sausage. How-ever, you can substitute unsalted butter for the drippings.

To make gravy: Discard all but 2 tablespoons of drippings (or melt 2 tablespoons unsalted butter) in the skillet. Stir in 2 tablespoons of the country gravy mix. Over low heat, cook about 2 minutes, stirring constantly. Whisk in 1 cup chicken broth, scraping browned bits off bottom of skillet. Stir in 1 cup milk and bring to a boil over high heat, stir-ring constantly. Reduce heat to low and simmer for about 5 minutes. Serve immediately with chicken, mashed potatoes, or biscuits. Makes 2 cups gravy.

Dry Onion Dip Mix

- ¾ c. dry minced onion
- ⅓ c. beef bouillon powder
- 4 t. onion powder
- ¼ t. crushed celery seed
- ¼ t. sugar

Combine all ingredients. Store in a container with a tight-fitting lid. About 5 tablespoons of mix are equal to one 1.25-ounce package.

To make onion dip: Combine 5 tablespoons mix with 1 pint sour cream.

Taco Seasoning Mix

2 t.   dry minced onion

1 t.   salt

1 t.   chili powder

½ t.   cornstarch

⅛ t.   crushed dried red pepper

½ t.   dry minced garlic

¼ t.   dried oregano

½ t.   ground cumin

Combine all ingredients. Store in a container with a tight-fitting lid.

To make taco filling: Brown 1½ pounds lean ground beef in a medium skillet over medium-high heat. Drain the fat. Add ½ cup water and 2 tablespoons taco seasoning mix. Reduce heat and simmer 10 minutes, stirring occasionally. Makes filling for 8 to10 tacos.

This recipe multiplies well but should be used within 6 months.

Chicken Coating Mix

4 c.   dry bread crumbs

⅓ c.   vegetable oil

1 T.   salt

1 T.   paprika

1 T.   celery salt

1 t.   ground black pepper

½ t.   garlic salt

½ t.   dry minced garlic

¼ t.   dry minced onion

1 pinch   dried basil

1 pinch   dried parsley

1 pinch   dried oregano

Combine all ingredients. Store in a container with a tight-fitting lid for up to 6 months in the pantry, longer in the refrigerator.

Like Rice-a-Roni

2 c.   raw rice (not instant or Minute Rice)

1 c.   broken vermicelli pasta pieces (find this in the
       pasta aisle)

¼ c.   dried parsley flakes

6 T.   chicken or beef bouillon, powder or granules

2 t.   onion powder

½ t.   garlic powder

¼ t.   dried thyme

Combine all ingredients.

To use: Place 1 cup mix and 2 tablespoons butter or margarine in a heavy saucepan with 2¼ cups water. Bring to a boil. Cover and reduce heat. Simmer for 15 minutes or until rice is tender.

Family-Friendly
Finger Foods

Chicken Nuggets

2 lb.   boneless, skinless chicken breasts cut into 1½- to
2-inch pieces or 1-inch strips

1½ c.   chicken coating mix (see page 316)

Moisten chicken pieces with water. Shake off excess water.
Place coating mix in a plastic bag. Shake 3 or 4 pieces at a
time with coating mix. Discard any remaining coating mix.
Place chicken pieces in a single layer in a foil-lined 10 x
15 baking pan. Bake at 400° F for 10-15 minutes or until
chicken is cooked through. Serve with ranch dressing or
the dipping sauces that follow.

Breaded Chicken Fingers

6   boneless, skinless chicken breasts cut into ½-inch strips

1   egg, beaten

1 c.   buttermilk

1½ t.   garlic powder

1 c.   all-purpose flour

1 c.   seasoned bread crumbs

1 t.   salt

1 t.   baking powder

1 quart   oil for frying

Place chicken strips in a large, resealable plastic bag. In a small bowl, mix the egg, buttermilk, and garlic powder. Pour mixture into bag with chicken. Seal and refrigerate 2–4 hours.

In another large, resealable plastic bag, combine flour, bread crumbs, salt, and baking powder. Remove chicken from refrigerator and drain, discarding buttermilk mixture. Place chicken in flour mixture bag. Seal and shake to coat.

Heat oil in a large, heavy skillet to 375° F. Place coated chicken in hot oil. Fry until golden brown and juices run clear, or about 7 minutes. Drain on paper towels.

Sweet and Sour Dipping Sauce

2 c.	water
⅔ c.	distilled white vinegar
1½ c.	white sugar
1 6-oz. can	tomato paste
1 8-oz. can	crushed pineapple, drained
3 T.	cornstarch

Combine all ingredients in a medium saucepan. Cook over medium heat, stirring occasionally, for 15 minutes or until mixture reaches desired color and consistency.

Honey Mustard Dipping Sauce

1½ c.	mayonnaise
¼ c.	Dijon mustard
½ c.	honey

Combine all ingredients in a medium bowl. Chill in the refrigerator at least 2 hours before serving.

Asian Dipping Sauce

¼ c. soy sauce

½ t. sesame oil

1 clove garlic, minced

1 t. green onions, chopped

1 T. water

2 T. hoisin sauce

¼ t. minced fresh ginger

½ t. white sugar

Combine all ingredients in a small mixing bowl. Add additional hoisin sauce to thicken mixture to desired consistency if needed. Cover the sauce and refrigerate for 1–2 hours to allow flavors time to blend. Heat before serving. Makes ¼ cup sauce. Recipe multiplies well.

Appendix B

I n the previous chapters, we talked about how to cut the cost of life's big expenses. But if you're not careful, all you don't spend on the big stuff will disappear on small stuff. What follows are ways to spend less money on everyday expenses.

Coffee

Home-Roasted Coffee

If you love good coffee but hate paying $15 to $20 a pound for high-quality coffee beans of marginal freshness, have I got great news. You can drink the best and pay half the price. The secret? Roast your own coffee beans. It's cheap, it's fun, and you'll be the envy of your friends and family. Try it a few times and you'll have a new hobby.

While there are several methods for roasting, the easiest is to roast beans outdoors in a popcorn popper, specifically a West Bend Poppery II air popper. If you don't have one stashed in your garage from years gone by, you can pick these up at garage sales and on eBay for just a few dollars. You will want to keep your coffee roasting popper for that purpose only. It will get quite grungy in time. Here's the least you need to know to get you roasting as soon as your beans arrive.

Plug in the machine. Pour ¾ cup green beans into the chamber. Place the top, including the butter-melting dish, in place. After a few minutes, you will hear the "first crack." The beans won't pop out like popcorn but will simply make a slight cracking noise from the heat building up inside them. You will notice the beans starting to turn brown if you lift the butter dish and peer into the chamber. Replace and allow to continue roasting.

After about five minutes from the start, you will hear the "second crack." Now you are at a light to medium roast—my personal favorite. If you wait six minutes (one popper will vary in temperature from another so the time may vary as well), you will have a full-bodied dark French roast. At this point, the beans begin to smoke, which is why you must roast outdoors. The fragrance does not smell at all like coffee, by the way.

Once you reach a dark roast, you must immediately unplug the popper and pour the beans into a colander. Actually, you need two so you can pour the beans back and forth to cool them quickly. If you've gone for a dark roast, they will smoke up a storm as you quickly cool them, and that's just fine. (You will know from the smell if you've gone too far and truly burned the coffee. But don't give up. Just toss it out and roast another batch.)

Theoretically, you can roast coffee in any vessel that gets very hot. A Whirley-Pop popcorn popper works well, as does a cast iron skillet. I've used both but only outdoors on the side burner of my barbecue grill. Both must be stirred manually and watched carefully. In my opinion, while you can roast more coffee at a time, the stir method is not as reliable or as easy as the air popcorn popper method.

Roasted beans should be allowed to mellow for at least two hours before grinding. Store beans in a tightly sealed container. Grind the beans in your coffee grinder as you would any beans you purchase from the supermarket or coffee shop.

And now for the good news. Green beans start as low as $5.75 a pound (at this writing), depending on the origin and variety. I'm a creature of habit and have become very fond of the La Minita Tarrazu coffee beans from Costa Rica. When the price is right, I order 25 to 50 pounds at a time.

If you find a good cup of coffee to be one of life's extraordinary joys, just wait until you make it from beans you've roasted yourself. It's very much like the difference between eating a vine-ripened tomato from your garden and eating one of those pinkish excuses for a tomato from the grocery store.

It takes an entire growing season to have luscious tomatoes, and they last for such a short time. But coffee? I can have it every day year-round. And I love serving really good coffee to my family and friends too. Coffee made from beans roasted at home is so economical that it tastes that much more delicious!

Coffee Resources

U-Roast-Em (URoastEm.com). This is a no-frills green coffee bean source. The prices are competitive, and the customer service is good. You'll find good information and personal attention at this site. You can purchase beans at a discount if you order 5 pounds at a time. However, you'll get better discounts if you order 25 pounds at a time. Not to worry. Green beans have a very long shelf life—up to a year, provided they are stored in an ordinary paper bag, cotton cloth bag, or burlap bag. Coffee needs to breathe so moisture cannot condense around it, so don't lock it up in an airtight vault, tomb, or cedar chest. Direct sunlight is not good either. Once roasted, coffee beans should be used within two weeks. Once ground, coffee should be used immediately.

Sweet Marias (SweetMarias.com). You will find terrific information in the library at this site. They also offer equipment, supplies, and green beans, but prices are typically higher than U-Roast-Em.

Fabric

You might find fabric to be an odd item to mention, until you discover that I am a lover of fabric. I am a sewer, quilter, and knitter. So of course you would expect me to have a couple of secrets up my sleeve. If you know your fabrics, I can direct you to some bargain resources.

The Fabric Shack (FabricShack.com). This website carries an extensive line of name-brand, first-quality fabrics: Moda, Bernatex, Hoffman, Nathan, Robert Kaufman, RJR, and P&B to name a few. While retail prices for high-quality yard goods vary from one region to another, I can count on this store to routinely price the items I want up to 50 percent off the best price locally. The service is excellent, fabrics are delivered with the greatest of care, and customer service is first class.

QuiltShops.com. Imagine visiting all 144 of the very best quilt shops in the US at the same time (be still my heart).

That's what you have if you go to QuiltShops.com. My favorite search on this site is to use the word "sale" followed by whatever I'm looking for. For example, I searched "sale flannel" and came up with 1,392 bolts of flannel on sale! Because I selected "thumbnail" as my view option, I had a swatch of each and every bolt on my computer screen for my consideration. Of course, that's far too many to comprehend, so I narrowed my search by adding "green." As I considered each possibility, I also checked out the particular quilt shop.

Even if I do not make a purchase, I stay current on what's hot, what's not, competitive prices, and how my local quilt shop stacks up against the competition nationwide. I often find exactly what I need on sale for 50 percent off or more. Of course, shipping and handling are a factor to be considered whenever buying by mail order.

Fabric.com. This is another of my mail-order favorites. But think of this as a gigantic warehouse where you'd better be wearing comfortable shoes because you're going to be there for a while. You'll have to dig for treasure, but when you find it, expect the price to be worth the effort. You'll find lots of name-brand home-decorating and upholstery fabrics as well as quilt, craft, and apparel fabrics. There's always a large selection of $2 per yard fabrics, sometimes even cheaper! The service here is reliable, but don't expect a lot of attention to detail when it comes to packing your shipment. But who cares when the price is so right?

Hancocks of Paducah (Hancocks-Paducah.com). Not to be confused with the chain of fabric stores called Hancocks, Hancocks of Paducah is the largest fabric store in the world. At least that's how it appeared to me when I visited several years ago. It is so huge and well organized that I was paralyzed with excitement. They have an excellent website with online ordering, a great catalog that is released quarterly, and top-of-the-line customer service. Regular prices are consistently 25 percent less than retail in my local quilt shop for the same high-quality fabric.

Books

Let me say I approach this topic with mixed emotions. On the one hand, I write books for my livelihood, and this only works if people actually buy my books. On the other hand, I must say I hope you did not pay full price for the one you now hold, or any others for that matter. There are several ways you can get books at deep discounts.

Amazon. Many of the books available at Amazon.com can be purchased "used" for considerably less than the cover price. You will see this option right at the book listing.

Half.com. Exactly as you might imagine, this is a website where you can find books for half the price. Expect previously owned books with exact condition clearly disclosed. Remarkably, you can find current bestsellers. You can also sell your gently used books at Half.com.

The downside of Half.com is that since the site is a kind of clearinghouse for many individual sellers, you need to be patient. Don't expect next-day delivery the way you might (for an additional fee) at a site like Amazon.com or BN.com. Also, watch the shipping and handling charges. If you opt for "media mail" delivery (cheap!), your book will arrive (someday) via the slowest method the US Postal Service can arrange. If you upgrade, you might unknowingly negate what you've saved. Just pay attention.

Library. Not every book you need to read is a book you need to own. There is no better place for you to find those books than at your local public library. And while you're there, look around and see everything else it offers. Not only can you borrow books, ebooks, videos, and audio books—even character cake pans and coffeemakers at some libraries I've heard from!—but you can also read your favorite magazines, attend a book signing, or join a reading group. All libraries are now equipped with computers and internet access as well.

Have you checked your library's website lately? Be prepared for a treat. More than likely you can search the library's catalog and even make a reservation for that hot, new bestseller. Can't find the book you need? Ask the librarian to get it for you through interlibrary loan. Or if it's a new title, request they add it to the library's collection with your name first on the list to borrow it.

Laundry Detergent

This may be my favorite way to save money. Yes, I make my own laundry detergent. I've used every kind of commercial product you can imagine and will say without hesitation that my homemade product beats anything out there. It has no perfumes or coloring. It is HE compliant (front-loading washers require high-efficiency or HE detergents only), easy to make, and, best of all, cheap.

To make one gallon of liquid laundry detergent, assemble the following.

A container. A one-gallon container with a tight-fitting lid is what you are looking for here. I use an empty Arrowhead water container.

Borax. Find this as 20 Mule Team Borax or any brand of borax in the laundry aisle of your supermarket or a department store like Walmart or Target.

Super Washing Soda or soda ash. Super Washing Soda by Arm & Hammer (sodium carbonate) is becoming increasingly difficult to find. If you can't find it in the laundry aisle somewhere close to the borax, consider using soda ash (sodium carbonate) instead. Soda ash is exactly the same thing as Super Washing Soda and is used in swimming pools to fix the pH. It's readily available in pool supply stores and is much cheaper than Super Washing Soda.

Blue Dawn. Yes, this would be the dishwashing liquid. There seem to be multiple versions of blue Dawn these days. I've seen the blue version sold as "Original," "Ultra Concentrated," and, most recently, "Advanced Power." I've tested all of them, and I can detect no difference in the final product we're going to make here. As long as it's blue and it's authentic Dawn—not some look-alike store or generic brand—use it. Currently, I am using blue Dawn Advanced Power because that is what Costco is stocking.

Three-fourths cup measuring device. If you don't have one that is exactly 3/4 cup, use a 1/2 cup and a 1/4 cup.

Next, follow these steps.

Step 1: Measure 3/4 cup borax and 3/4 cup Super Washing Soda (or soda ash) and pour both into the empty one-gallon container.

Step 2: Add about 2 or 3 cups of the hottest water you have available from the tap. You'll see a few bubbles form but nothing to be concerned about.

Step 3: Apply the lid and shake the container vigorously until the powdered ingredients dissolve and the solution looks milky.

Step 4: Fill the container with hot water to within about an inch of the top, more or less depending on the shape of your container. You want to leave enough room for the Dawn.

Step 5: Pour in ¾ cup blue Dawn dishwashing liquid. Do this slowly so you don't create a lot of suds or bubbles.

Step 6: Once you've poured in all of the Dawn, fill the measuring cup with more hot water so you can top off the container and rinse out the last of the Dawn. If you still have room, add more water until you are about ½ inch from the top.

Step 7: Apply the lid. This should be quite easy because you will not be contending with suds or bubbles. Notice how the Dawn is not fully mixed up. That's fine. Just get that lid on tightly.

Step 8: Instead of shaking it, lay the container on its side and roll it around a bit to get everything mixed.

Take a moment to admire your beautiful homemade product and then get to the laundry room, where you will need your gallon of laundry detergent and a ¼ cup.

Measure out ¼ cup detergent. Pour it in the way you have always added detergent to your washer. If you have a detergent dispenser, that's where this ¼ cup of beautiful liquid goes.

If you're like me, your first thought is, "That cannot possibly be enough!" But it is. My washer is a top-loading HE by LG with Wave Force. It's quite possibly the best washing machine I have ever used in my life. One-quarter cup of this detergent does the trick.

If you use more than ¼ cup per load, you can expect a couple of things to happen. Your clothes will come out of the dryer scratchy and stiff, and after a while you will notice your white items turning a lovely shade of pale gray. That's the sign of too much detergent left in the clothes. If you just cannot bear to use only ¼ cup of detergent, make sure you double rinse.

This detergent is absolutely low sudsing, which is what HE washers require. However, if you do not have an HE machine, this detergent is still fabulous for your traditional washer.

Remember that I used the Dawn Advanced Power. Well, guess what? Something new happened that did not happen with the Ultra Dawn. I'm not sure why, and it seems not to be a problem at all, but after an hour or so, the Dawn separates and floats to the top of the container. So I just give it a good shake or roll before each use.

Shampoo

Come on . . . 'fess up. You feel guilty using $0.99 shampoo because it's really bad for your hair and the $24 variety at the salon is so much better, especially for chemically treated hair. Right? Wrong!

Some cheap shampoos are wonderful, and some $24 varieties have all the gentleness of a can of scouring powder. Price has nothing to do with quality.

All shampoos regardless of the brand are 80 to 90 percent water. The rest is detergent with a pathetically few drops of fragrance and other additives and preservatives. There are basically two kinds of detergent: anionic (harsh) and cationic (gentle). The only part of the shampoo bottle that's regulated by the Food and Drug Administration (FDA) is the list of ingredients. Manufacturers can and do make any claim they like on the unregulated portions of the label. Sometimes the hype has some merit; often it has none.

Pay no attention to anything on the bottle or packaging except for the list of ingredients. Water (or some fancy name for good old H2O) will always be the first ingredient. Next comes the detergent. Examples you can expect to find are:

Ammonium Lauryl Sulfate—very harsh

Ammonium Laureth Sulfate—harsh

Sodium Lauryl Sulfate (SLS)—still harsh

Sodium Laureth Sulfate (SLES)—mild, great choice

TEA (or MEA) Lauryl Sulfate—gentle, good choice

TEA (or MEA) Laureth Sulfate—gentle, good choice

Shampoos often contain antistatic and detangling agents and also thickeners, humectants (moisturizers), and conditioners. But these items are in such small quantities it's almost a joke. Besides, the detergent washes all of it down the drain when you rinse.

You will find several popular shampoo brands that contain the mild and gentle detergents (i.e., Herbal Essence). If you clip the shampoo coupons from your Sunday newspaper and then watch for shampoo sales in your grocery store, you will never pay more than $1 a bottle again.

Finally, don't go for the lather. Use only a quarter-size amount of shampoo—that's all it takes. Interestingly, the "rinse and repeat" instruction you read on every shampoo bottle goes back to a marketing campaign one manufacturer came up with to increase sales. It does that all right. You can make your shampoo last twice as long if you simply do not repeat.

Conditioner

With some of the money you don't spend on shampoo, buy a quality conditioner. While not a foolproof way to measure quality when it comes to conditioner, I find that price is a good indicator. Spend a bit more and you'll get better quality. And as a bonus, the higher the quality, the less you need to use. So maybe the pricier option is more cost-effective after all.

Notes

Chapter 2: Found Money

1. www.gallup.com/poll/22879/Credit-Card-Owners-Average-Balance-More-Than-3000.aspx.

2. blog.nsbank.com/are-you-spending-more-than-you-earn-19-of-americans-are/ and www.usfinancialcapability.org/results.php?region=US.

3. Adam Smith, *The Wealth of Nations*, Google eBook, Digireads .com, January 1, 2004, 21, http://books.google.com/books?id=rBiqT86B GQEC&pg=PA21&lpg=PA21&dq="The+real+price+of+everything,+ what+everything+really+costs+to+the+man+who+wants+to+acquire +it,+is+the+toil+and+trouble+of+acquiring+it."&source=bl&ots=Zz -dUbTKTV&sig=axGyUIqgCIKhtLxR_Vp1rsr9TqU&hl=en&sa=X& ei=PITyU9k3z_WgBOmigfgH&ved=0CCsQ6AEwAg#v=onepage&q= "The%20real%20price%20of%20everything%2C%20what%20every thing%20really%20costs%20to%20the%20man%20who%20wants%20 to%20acquire%20it%2C%20is%20the%20toil%20and%20trouble%20 of%20acquiring%20it."&f=false.

Chapter 3: Handy Tools, Secret Weapons

1. Privacy Pitfalls in No-Swipe Credit Cards, Slashdot, http://beta. slashdot.org/story/06/10/23/0512204/privacy-pitfalls-in-no-swipe-credit-cards; www.cnbc.com/id/101187512#.

2. For Merchants | MasterCard®, www.mastercard.com/ca/merchant/en/getstarted/value.html.

3. http://online-auction-sites.toptenreviews.com.

Chapter 4: The Jarring Truth about Food Shopping

1. www.cnpp.usda.gov/sites/default/files/usda_food_plans_cost_of_food/CostofFoodJan2014.pdf.

Chapter 5: News Flash! There's a Kitchen in Your House

1. www.ers.usda.gov/publications/aib-agricultural-information-bulletin/aib792-4.aspx#.U7MUq8bGNNs.

2. United States Department of Agriculture, Agriculture Information Bulletin Number 790, July 2004, www.ers.usda.gov/media/303041/aib790_1_.pdf.

3. www.sdearthtimes.com/et0598/et0598s10.html.

Chapter 8: Attack of the Killer Fees

1. www.huffingtonpost.com/2013/03/29/overdraft-fees_n_2980946.html.

Chapter 9: Home, Sweet, Paid-for Home

1. http://ycharts.com/indicators/us_existing_singlefamily_home_median_sales_price.

Chapter 10: Remember When Talk Was Cheap?

1. www.pewinternet.org/fact-sheets/mobile-technology-fact-sheet/.

2. http://arstechnica.com/business/2014/01/verizon-leads-top-wireless-carriers-in-bill-size-at-148-a-month/.

3. http://blogs.wsj.com/economics/2013/09/05/about-1-in-3-households-has-no-landline-phone/.

4. Ibid.

5. Porting means taking your current phone number away from the current provider and transporting it to another carrier.

Chapter 11: Strategies for Big-Ticket Items

    1. www.internetworldstats.com/am/us.htm.

Chapter 13: Disaster, Disease, Death, and Other Fun Topics

    1. www.cars.com/go/advice/Story.jsp?section=ins&subject=ins_req&story=state-insurance-requirements.

Index

3-year rule, 177, 214
5 A Day for Better
   Health, 95
5 Dollar Dinners, 102
80–percent rule, 270
80–20 rule, 119
911, mobile phone, 167

AAA, 216, 225
Affordable Care Act,
   the, 229
AirlineConsolidators.
   com, 246
airline fares, 241
air travel, 241
ALDI, 84
Allrecipes.com, 100
Amazon.com, 180
Amazon Prime, 173
Amazon, 328
antenna, TV, 172
Apple TV, 173
appliances
   floor models, 183
   home, 182
   obsolescence, built-in,
   177

Asian Dipping Sauce, 322
ATM fees, 143
attitude, 60
auction houses, 186
auctions, online, 135
auto, best time to shop,
   215
auto, history report, 209
auto insurance require-
   ments by state, 224
automobile, late model,
   low mileage, 204
automobile, rules for
   buying at half the
   price, 201
automobile lease, 217

bakery outlets, 85
bank, local independent,
   144
bank, penalty fees, 149
bank accounts, 142, 144
Barker, Bob, 276
Beef Gravy Mix, 311
big-ticket items, 175
BJ's, 83, 168, 183, 216, 247
Blasted Chicken, 281

BookingBuddy, 245
Borax, 330
Breaded Chicken Fingers,
   320
Brite-View, 173
Brown Rice, 294

Cake Mix Cookies, 302
cake mixes, 93
California Farm Bureau
   Federation, 230
car, history report, 209
Cars.com, 224
cash, 45
catastrophic insurance,
   229
CellTradeUSA.com, 169
CFBF.com, 230
Cheap Cooking, 74
CheapTickets.com, 246
Chicken and Beef Broth,
   296
Chicken Coating Mix,
   316
Chicken Gravy Mix, 312
Chicken Nuggets, 319
children's museums, 257

claims, insurance, 221
closet sweep, 127
collision insurance, 228
Color Me Beautiful, 122
community-supported
    agriculture, 87
complain, how to, 261
comprehensive insurance,
    228
computers, 189
conditioner, 334
consignment shops, 57,
    128, 131–32, 134,
    138–39, 186
Consumer Reports,
    179–80, 183, 214
cookbooks, 100
Costco, 83, 168, 183, 188,
    216, 231, 247, 330
Country Gravy Mix, 313
Coupon Mom, 79
credit card
    accounts, 147
    complaints, 265
    fee-free, 148
    interest rates, 147
    late payment fees, 147
    overlimit fees, 147
    service fees, 147
credit score, 55, 222
credit union, 144
Crock-Pot, 97–99
CSA, 87
Cut Out Hunger, 79

Dansko outlet, 132
Dawn, blue, 330
deal alternatives, 216
dealer's invoice, 213
debit cards, 54
Debt-Proof Living, 271
deductible, insurance, 227
department stores, dis-
    count, 135
Designer Cuisine, create
    your own, 305
digital tuner, 172

directory assistance, free,
    171
discount department
    stores, 135
discounters, deep, 134
discount warehouse clubs,
    83, 183, 188
Dollar Stretcher, 74
dry cleaners complaints,
    264
Dry Onion Dip Mix, 314
DVR, 173

early termination fees,
    169, 217
eating out, 104
eBid.com, 58
eMeals, 101
Energy Star, 184
envelopes, 48
ePier.com, 58
Epinions.com, 180
equity, home, 152
estate sales, 186
Expedia, 244

Fabric.com, 327
fabric resources, 326
Fabric Shack, the, 326
factory tours, 255–57
FactoryToursUSA.com,
    257
family vacations, 255
fare bases, 241
Farm Bureau, health in-
    surance, 230–31
Federal Reserve Board,
    265
FICO, 55
financing, auto, 215
First MSA, 230
FirstMSA.com, 230
Food 4 Less, 83
FRB.gov, 265
freezer-ready, 93
frequent flier clubs, 247
FTC.gov, 264
furniture, 185

garden, 86
gardens, community, 87
gifting, strategic, 138
Google Shopping, 181
GotApex.com, 190
groceries, two methods
    shopping for, 71
grocery co-ops, 87
Grocery Game, the, 78
grocery store, no frills, 83
ground beef, freezing, 302

Half.com, 328
Hancocks of Paducah,
    327
hand-me-downs, 138
health insurance, 229
health savings accounts,
    230
high-deductible insurance,
    229
HighPointFurnitureSales.
    com, 185
history report, auto, 209
homeowner's insurance,
    234
homeownership, 151
Home-Roasted Coffee,
    323
Honey Mustard Dipping
    Sauce, 321
hotels, 249
Hotwire, 245
HSA, 230
Hulu, 173
Hy-Vee, 83

IFI.org, 264
IIHS.org, 223
insurance
    catastrophic, 229
    cell phone, 169
    health, 299
    homeowner's, 234
    life, 232
insurance claims, 221
insurance complaints, 264
insurance discount, 227

insurance guidelines, 220
Insurance Institute for
  Highway Safety, 223
internet channels, streaming, 173

Kayak.com, 243
kits, unfinished, 186

landline, 166–67
laundry detergent,
  recipe, 329
LearnVest, 49
lease, auto, 217
libraries, 329
life insurance, 232–33
living history museums,
  257
long-distance calling, 167
lunch at work, 107

Magnavox, 173
markets, farmer's, 86
Marshalls, 134
Master Biscuit Mix, 297
mattresses, 187
meal replacements, 105
mechanic, reputable, 208
minimum balance fees,
  143
Mint, 49
mobile virtual network
  operators, 169
Mobissimo, 245
MoneyFactory.com, 257
MoneySpot.org, 74
mortgage, rapid repay-
  ment, 154
mortgage refinancing, 159
MSA Bank, 230
MSAbank.com, 230
MSRP, auto, 216
Muffin Mix, 292
museums
  children's, 257
  living history, 257
  Washington, DC, 257
MVNOs, 169

National Cancer Insti-
  tute, 95
National Writer's Asso-
  ciation, 231
nationalwriters.com, 231
needs shopping, 71
negotiation, power of, 64
Netflix, 173
new car, how to buy, 210
no, power of, 63

Once Upon a Child, 138
OnlineAuction.com, 58
online auctions, 135
Orange Muffins, 290
Orbitz, 244
organic, 86–87
Organized Home, 74
OshKosh, 139
OshKoshBGosh.com, 139
OUAC.com, 138
outlets, clothing, 132
overdraft fees, 143

Pak'n Save, 83
pay ahead, 156
pay down, 156
Perfect Pasta, 295
personal finance, 10 rules
  of, 268
phone cards, prepaid, 168
pillow-top mattress, 188
Playstation 4, 173
price book, 73
Priceline, 246
prices, compare, 181
PrimeDTV, 174
property taxes, 152
published fare, 242

Quick and Easy Stir-Fry,
  284
QuiltShops.com, 326

Rapid Debt-Repayment
  Plan, 240
refinancing mortgage, 159

rental car insurance, 252
rental cars, 252
rental returns, 187
reserve shopping, 71–73
Rice-a-Roni, Like, 317
Roku, 173
Ross, 134
rules of personal finance,
  268

SalesCircular.com, 183
Sam's Club, 83, 168, 183,
  188, 216, 234, 247
scratch and dent, 83, 184
search engines, travel, 245
secondary market, 57
self-talk, 62
semi-fast food, 113
Sensational Rice, 282
ShakerWorkshops.com,
  187
shampoo, 332
shape, body, 123
SiriusXM Internet Radio,
  173
slow cooker, 97–98
smart TV, 173
Smith, Adam, 39
software, 49
specials of the house, 96
SpeedyPin.com, 170
staples, grocery, 91
Stein Mart, 134
stir-fry, 99
stockpile, 71
Stretcher.com, 74
StyleMakeovers.com, 122
supermarket alterna-
  tives, 83
supermarkets, green, 85
Super Washing Soda, 330
Sweet and Sour Dipping
  Sauce, 321
Sweet Marias, 326

Taco Seasoning Mix, 315
tailor, 130

temperaments, money, 37
The Pocket Stylist, 123
Three Packets and a
  Cluck, 287
Three Packets and a Moo,
  286
Three Packets and an
  Oink, 288
three-year rule, 177
thrift stores, 133–34, 186
ticket consolidators, 246
ticket splitting, 249
TiVo, 173
T.J. Maxx, 134
tracking, 55
trade association, health
  insurance, 231
traffic school, 226
travel, air, 241
travel agencies, online,
  244
travel agents, 247
Travelocity, 244
travel search engines, 245
Truth or Consequences,
  276
two price tags, big-ticket
  items, 178

umbrella insurance, 236
unfinished kits, 186
uniform, 120
U-Roast-Em, 325
USAA.com, 149
USAA Federal Savings
  Bank, 144

USAA insurance, 224
used car, how to buy, 206

vacations, family, 255
Vandykes.com, 187
variable vs. fixed inter-
  est, 162
Verizon wireless, 165
VIN, 209
VOIP, 166

Walmart, 84
wardrobe plan
  boy's, 137
  career man, 127
  career woman, 126
  girl's, 137
warranties, extended, 190
water heater, 237
WeBidz.com, 58
WebStore.com, 58
White Rice, 293
wireless, 168–69
wireless service com-
  plaints, 264

Xbox One, 173

YNAB, 50

Recipes

Asian Dipping Sauce, 322
Beef Gravy Mix, 311
Blasted Chicken, 281
Breaded Chicken Fingers,
  320

Brown Rice, 294
Cake Mix Cookies, 302
Chicken and Beef Broth,
  296
Chicken Coating Mix,
  316
Chicken Gravy Mix, 312
Chicken Nuggets, 319
Country Gravy Mix, 313
designer cuisine, create
  your own, 305
Dry Onion Dip Mix, 314
ground beef, freezing, 302
Honey Mustard Dipping
  Sauce, 321
Master Biscuit Mix, 297
master recipes, 293
Muffin Mix, 292
Orange Muffins, 290
Perfect Pasta, 295
Quick and Easy Stir-Fry,
  284
Rice-a-Roni, Like, 317
Sensational Rice, 282
Sweet and Sour Dipping
  Sauce, 321
Taco Seasoning Mix, 315
Three Packets and a
  Cluck, 287
Three Packets and a Moo,
  286
Three Packets and an
  Oink, 288
White Rice, 293

Mary Hunt, award-winning and bestselling author, syndicated columnist, and sought-after motivational speaker, has created a global platform that is making strides to help men and women battle the epidemic impact of consumer debt. Mary is the founder of Debt-Proof Living, a highly regarded organization consisting of an interactive website, a monthly newsletter, a daily syndicated column, and hundreds of thousands of loyal followers. Since 1992, DPL has been dedicated to its mission to provide hope, help, and realistic solutions for individuals who are committed to financially responsible and debt-free living.

As a speaker, Mary travels extensively, addressing conferences, corporations, colleges, universities, and churches at home and abroad. A frequent guest on radio and television, she has appeared on dozens of television shows, including *Dr. Phil*, *Good Morning America*, *The Oprah Winfrey Show*, and *Dateline*.

Mary lives with her husband in Orange County, California.

Debt-Proof LIVING

Debt-Proof Living is a great big wonderful community offering help and hope to anyone who wants to learn how to manage their money more effectively. If you want to get out of debt—or stay out—and learn how to live below your means, Debt-Proof Living is the place to be.

Debt-proof living is a way of life where you spend less than you earn; you give and save consistently; your financial decisions are purposeful; and you work toward your goals by following a specific plan.

DebtProofLiving.com is the home of the debt-proof living philosophy. It is primarily a member-only website with features ranging from money management tools, articles, resources, community forums, consumer tips, recipes, and more. Here you'll find, in continuous publication since 1992, the DPL newsletter, which is published in an online format available to all members of this website.

Visit DebtProofLiving.com today to find out how you can debt-proof your life!